TWELVE STEP
CHRISTIANITY

TWELVE STEP CHRISTIANITY

THE CHRISTIAN ROOTS AND APPLICATION OF THE TWELVE STEPS

Saul Selby

Hazelden
Publishing

HAZELDEN
PITTMAN
Archives
Press

Hazelden Publishing
Center City, Minnesota 55012-0176
hazelden.org/bookstore

Library of Congress Cataloging-in-Publication Data
Selby, Saul, 1952–
  Twelve step Christianity : the Christian roots and application of the twelve steps /
Saul Selby.
      p.cm.
  Includes bibliographical references.
  ISBN 1-56838-561-7 (pbk.)
    1. Twelve-step programs—Religious aspects—Christianity. 2. Spiritual life—
Christianity. I. Title.
  BV4596.T88 S45 2000
  248.8'629—dc21   00-044995

28 27 26 25 24   13 14 15 16 17

Editor's note

The Twelve Steps are reprinted with permission of Alcoholics Anonymous World
Services, Inc. (AAWS). Permission to reprint the Twelve Steps does not mean that
AAWS has reviewed or approved the contents of this publication, or that AAWS neces-
sarily agrees with the views expressed herein. AA is a program of recovery from alcoholism *only*—use of the Twelve Steps in connection with other problems, or in any
other non-AA context, does not imply otherwise. Although Alcoholics Anonymous
is a spiritual program, AA is not a religious program, and use of AA material in the
present connection does not imply AA's affiliation with or endorsement of any sect,
denomination, or specific religious belief.

   All the stories in this book are based on actual experiences. In certain cases, names
and details have been changed to protect the privacy of the people involved. In some
cases, composites have been created.

   All Bible quotations are from the New American Standard Version, unless otherwise noted.

Cover design by David Spohn
Interior design by Nora Koch / Gravel Pit Publications
Typesetting by Nora Koch / Gravel Pit Publications

CONTENTS

INTRODUCTION

Changed lives validated Jesus' ministry when He walked the earth two thousand years ago. He healed the sick, cast out demons, forgave the unforgivable, and freed those in bondage to sin. When disciples of John the Baptist wanted to know if Jesus was the "Expected One," Jesus pointed to changed lives as proof of His calling. He said:

> Go and report to John what you have seen and heard: the blind receive sight, the lame walk, the lepers are cleansed, and the deaf hear, the dead are raised up, the poor have the gospel preached to them. And blessed is he who keeps from stumbling over Me.[1]

Nothing has changed. Jesus continues to radically change lives just as He did two thousand years ago. Today His life-changing power regularly transforms hopeless addicts into sober role models, angry spouses into joyous individuals, thieves into philanthropists, sinners into saints, and religious hypocrites into people of love and integrity. His gracious mercy is limited only by one thing: our hearts and minds.

Jesus wants us to be free. Free to perform His will unhindered in a world of competing values. Free from fears, free from thoughts that distract us from His purpose, free from a lifestyle that has no meaning, free from addictions and habits which hold us prisoner, and, most important, free from sins that separate us from Him.

Christ's freedom is rarely experienced today. Twenty-first-century Christianity has unfortunately blended the "American dream" with the directives of Jesus and effectively muted out the life-changing freedom that Christ would have us enjoy. American-dream Christianity allows us to claim a relationship with Christ and rarely give a second thought to God's designed purpose for our lives. We seek comfort and ease and assume that this is God's will for us.

The freedom that Jesus offers is available to all but comes at a cost: our lives. Jesus says we must lose our life to find it.[2] To experience Christ's freedom we must voluntarily become His servant. We must willingly seek His purpose for our lives and discard any personal goals and ambitions that compete with His. It is the surrendered life that brings freedom.

Twelve Step Christianity is designed to help you lose your life so you may find it, through a biblical application of Alcoholics Anonymous's Twelve Steps. These Steps, when applied from a Christian perspective, are dynamic tools that enable individuals to experience Christ in a new, powerful, and life-changing way. They effectively guide us into a "surrendered" lifestyle that provides the healing and freedom that God has designed for us.

The Steps' effectiveness has nothing to do with AA's program but with Christ's commandments. Jesus advocated the core spiritual disciplines of repentance, self-examination,

---

1. Luke 7:18–23
2. Matt. 10:39

vii

confession, restitution, prayer, and witnessing long before AA existed, yet these disciplines are frequently ignored within the lives of Christians.

It would be an unfortunate mistake to assume this book is exclusively for addicts or individuals with major life problems. It certainly will assist addicts or anyone struggling with self-defeating or destructive behaviors. But this book's message is targeted for any Christian who desires an intimate relationship with Christ. Why? Because the Christian practices outlined by the Steps are desperately needed in believers' lives today. Contemporary Christians need to make their faith genuine. They need a sense of purpose other then simply existing. They need to experience Christ's love and power in their day-to-day lives. They need to demonstrate Christ's character as a testimony of God's reality to others. The biblical principles outlined in these Steps enable us to do that and more.

CHAPTER ONE

ARE THE STEPS JUST FOR ADDICTS?

Not all church buildings are alike. My first church met in a small, run-down movie theater in rural Minnesota. The faithful dutifully swept away piles of spilled popcorn and empty cups every Sunday morning. Floors coated with sticky soda pop routinely caused our feet to squeak as we prepared for the morning service.

This picture of church might not fit for some folks, but as a new Christian I was thrilled to be a part of it. My only expectation of church was a place where I could commune with God, experience Him in a real and powerful way. Stained-glass windows, oak pews, and a vaulted ceiling weren't important; cleaning a sticky mess wasn't a big deal; growing in a relationship with Christ was all that mattered.

Besides, I had nothing to compare it to. Church attendance was never on my list of things to do while growing up in New York City. As a nonreligious Jew I had no interest in syna-gogue or God, let alone church and Jesus Christ.

One Sunday morning I noticed Ron, a church leader, laughing uncontrollably while reading a church bulletin. "What's so funny?" I inquired. Ron gleefully directed me to the bulletin's description of next week's special speaker. It read: "Saul Selby, Jewish drug addict atheist from New York City will be sharing next week's message." The bulletin neglected to mention that I was no longer addicted to drugs and was now a believer in Jesus Christ. Few Jewish, drug-addicted atheists would be welcomed speakers in a church unless of course Christ had radical-ly transformed them.

That's exactly what had happened to me. God graciously transformed me from a hopeless addict to a hopeful believer. He removed my obsession to use drugs and alcohol and replaced it with a burning desire to serve His son—Jesus Christ. God had accomplished these changes through two primary sources: the Twelve Steps of AA and the Bible.

The Twelve Steps were introduced to me in addiction treatment as the cure for the curse of my addiction. Because I was an atheist who had contempt for the idea of God, the Twelve Steps made no sense. But as a desperate addict I was willing to try anything to overcome my addiction.

Begrudgingly, only out of fear and desperation, I tried applying these Steps. My efforts began with a simple and sincere prayer: "God, if you're real, make yourself real to me." To my surprise, my prayer was answered in a dramatic way. I immediately sensed a warm, comforting presence surrounding me. It replaced my fear with hope and assured me of God's reality. Despite my addicted lifestyle God graciously invited me into a relationship with Him.

Next, God used the Steps to draw me to Christ. As I sought through prayer and meditation to improve my understanding of God,[1] I found myself attracted to Jesus.

To understand Christ's message firsthand, I began to read the Bible. Christ's words spoke to me with authority. They exposed my sin, confirmed God's love, and directed me into a life-changing relationship with Him. Through His word, Jesus has became my savior, my Lord, and my friend.

Today, I find myself with one foot in two camps. As an addiction professional I regularly teach the Twelve Steps as a vehicle to recovery from addiction. As the director of a jail ministry I regularly challenge inmates to seek Christ as a resource for life and change. As a Christian who practices the Steps, I know them to be an invaluable tool to live out the Christian faith.

Many Christians misunderstand the Steps' purpose because the Steps have become stigmatized as a cure for addictive behavior alone. The thinking goes something like this: "If you have a headache, take aspirin. If your ankle is swollen, apply ice. If you're addicted, take the Twelve Steps." Plus, in some pockets of Christianity the Steps have been labeled as secular or worse yet—evil.

The spiritual ideals that the Steps embrace are neither evil nor were designed exclusively for addicts. They are scriptural principles that when acted upon, enhance our relationship with Christ.

The Steps are biblical. Each Step reflects spiritual principles that come directly out of the Bible.

Do the Steps enable recovery from addiction? Absolutely! If followed closely, they provide freedom to those suffering addiction's bondage. But the source of that power is a by-product of a life devoted to God—which is the Steps' primary purpose.

Christians in Twelve Step recovery programs will benefit from this book because it connects faith with the program. Each Step will be discussed from a biblical perspective. But this book is not just for Christians in recovery—it's for any Christian who desires an intimate relationship with Christ because the Steps are foundational elements of genuine Christianity. If you want to be close to Jesus, to do his will daily—if you want a sense of hope and purpose that comes from knowing and following Christ—read on.

---

1. This is Step Eleven.

CHAPTER TWO

WHAT IS TWELVE STEP CHRISTIANITY?

Nearly two billion people in the world consider themselves to be Christians—but why? By what standards do they identify themselves in this way? Answering this question is no easy task. Reasons why a person would declare oneself Christian could fill an entire book. Some proclaim, "I'm Christian because I prayed that Jesus would come into my heart." Others say, "I'm Christian because I was baptized." Others declare, "I'm Christian because I belong to a church." Still others, "I'm Christian because I was confirmed."

While all of these reasons are important, none seems to match the defining elements of Christianity that its author, Jesus Christ, proposed: to hear His voice, to follow Him, and to be known by Him.[1]

Our relationship with Jesus defines genuine Christianity. No salvation prayer, church membership, or baptism can ever substitute for intimate communion with Jesus Himself. Jesus desires His followers to imitate Him in word and deed. Jesus denied himself—so must His followers. Jesus put God's will ahead of His own—so must His followers. Jesus carried His cross—so must His followers. Jesus says, "Whoever does not carry his own cross and come after Me cannot be My disciple."[2] Yet, how many professing Christians truly seek and experience this relationship?

---

1. See John 10:27.
2. Luke 14:27

3

Many church members know *about* Jesus, but they don't *know Him*. They have been taught He existed, He died, He rose from the dead; and they believe it all. They have been told of His love, His power to forgive, and His eventual return. But they don't experience His love, care, and intimate touch in their lives. They don't daily seek His direction or desire to make sacrifices based on His will.

In a world focused on self-fulfillment and self-gratification, the challenges of Jesus are easily and routinely ignored. They are frequently replaced with subtle rationalizations that allow us to label ourselves Christians, yet not truly follow the One we identify ourselves with. It is far easier to wear a cross than to carry one, to quote Him than to follow Him, to deny our sins than to deny ourselves, to know about Him than to know Him.

Twelve Step Christianity is a process by which we totally surrender our lives to Christ. When applied from a Christian perspective, the spiritual principles outlined in the Steps direct us to seek His will (hear His voice) and submit to it (follow Him). The outcome is intimate communion with our Great Shepherd (being known by Him). These principles are simple, powerful, and completely consistent with Christ's teachings.

This is no coincidence. As we explore the history of the Steps we will find that their roots are biblical, developed by devout followers of Christ who sought with all their heart to follow Him. Just as these Christian principles worked for early Christians, they can work for us! When applied zealously, they enable us to become faithful followers of the Good Shepherd.

CHAPTER THREE

THE CHRISTIAN ROOTS OF THE TWELVE STEPS

We already had the basic ideas, though not in terse and tangible form. We got them, as I said, as a result of our study of the Good Book.[1]

(Dr. Robert Smith describing Alcoholics Anonymous's development of the Twelve Steps)

Though he could not accept all the tenets of the Oxford Groups, he [Bill Wilson] was convinced of the need for moral inventory, confession of personality defects, restitution to those harmed, helpfulness to others, and the necessity of belief in and dependence upon God.[2]

Bill Wilson, the cofounder of AA, penned the Twelve Steps, but he did not create them. Bill wrote the Steps, relying upon the spiritual principles he learned in the Oxford Group. This chapter will review the Christian roots of AA and the Steps by examining the program that Bill found sobriety in and eventually split away from—the Oxford Group.

In 1934 Bill was desperately seeking answers to his drinking problem. While hospitalized for the third time for alcoholism, he cried out to God for assistance. That prayer ignited a remarkable spiritual experience that transformed Bill's life and lifted his obsession to drink. It changed the

drunk Bill into the sober Bill; it changed the agnostic Bill into the believing Bill.

Bill recognized that his newfound sobriety was both precious and fragile. Its permanence, he reasoned, depended on a sustained relationship with God, who graciously met Bill in his time of need. He found the spiritual direction he needed not in AA (it did not yet exist), but in the Oxford Group.

The Oxford Group was a nondenominational Christian movement whose purpose was to lead individuals into a dynamic, life-changing relationship with Jesus Christ. The Oxford Group tenets proclaimed that God was more than just

---

1. *The Cofounders of Alcoholics Anonymous. Biographical Sketches, Their Last Major Talks* (New York: Alcoholics Anonymous World Services, 1972, 1975), 10.
2. *Alcoholics Anonymous*, 3d ed. (New York: Alcoholics Anonymous World Services, 1976), xvi.

an idea. God was a living spirit able to transform lives through personal contact with Him. Oxford Group members shared a burning desire to make their faith in Christ practical, dynamic, and real.

The Oxford Group was successful in helping alcoholics, but sobriety was not its designed purpose. Sobriety was just a by-product of the Oxford Group's goal of complete surrender of one's life to Christ. Like Bill, many alcoholics in the Oxford Group found that their obsession to drink vanished as Christ's power flowed into their lives.

It was this sobriety-producing power that Bill desperately sought and found through the Oxford Group's program and fellowship.

THE OXFORD GROUP'S CONTRIBUTION TO THE STEPS

The Oxford Group's founder, Frank Buchman, was largely responsible for its spiritual principles. It was through his own conversion experience that the vision of the Oxford Group, and ultimately the Steps, were spawned.

Buchman, a Lutheran minister, worked in a hospice for children. He loved his work, but his employment was cut short when he resigned following a dispute with the hospice's board of directors. He was a broken man. Filled with self-pity and resentment at his ex-employer, Buchman had little direction and was extremely discouraged. In an attempt to seek answers, he began to travel.

While in Europe, Buchman visited the Keswick Convention. Keswick, an annual Christian convention, was designed to spiritually edify those attending. For Buchman it did that and more.

While listening to a message by Jessie Penn-Lewis, Buchman was permanently changed.

Her message was simple, yet profound. Mel B. captures the essence of Penn-Lewis's message and Buchman's life-changing experience.

Jessie Penn-Lewis was no spellbinding orator, but that afternoon she had the power to help Buchman face the pride and bitterness that were destroying him. A. J. Russell noted that "in her simple, straight-forward, conversational talk . . . [she] spoke about the Cross of Christ, of the sinner and the One who had made full satisfaction for the sins of the world."

Buchman later said that this had been "a doctrine which I knew as a boy which my church believed, which I had always been taught and which that day became a great reality for me. I had entered the little church with a divided will, nursing pride, selfishness, ill-will, which prevented me from functioning as a Christian minister should. The woman's simple talk personalized the Cross for me that day, and suddenly I had a poignant vision of the Crucified.

"There was infinite suffering on the face of the Master, and I realized for the first time the great abyss separating myself from Him," Buchman later said. "That was all. But it produced in me a vibrant feeling, as though a strong current of life had suddenly been poured into me, and afterwards a dazed sense of a great spiritual shaking-up. There was no longer this feeling of a divided will, no sense of calculation and argument, of oppression and helplessness; a wave of strong emotion, following the will to surrender, rose up within me from the depths of an estranged spiritual life, and seemed to lift my soul from its anchorage of selfishness, bearing it across the great sundering abyss to the foot of the Cross."[3]

Buchman simultaneously received a revelation of Christ's love and of sin's power. His selfishness, pride, and self-pity were exposed as ugly sin, which had succeeded in distancing him from Christ. Furthermore his sin prevented him from understanding and following whatever plan God had for him. He knew that he must repent and surrender his life totally to God.

He followed this new insight with action. He immediately wrote letters of apology to his board of directors, acknowledging his unfair judgment of them and asking for their forgiveness. His self-pity and resentment were now replaced with hope, vitality, and a burning desire to seek and accomplish God's will daily.

Buchman was convinced that his situation was not unique. He believed that many professing Christians lacked the fulfillment and purpose that God had planned for them and that both denied and unconfessed sins dominated their lives.

He became determined to lead others into this life-changing process. His efforts eventually led to the development of the Oxford Group, which quickly became an international organization. Following are some of the Oxford Group's spiritual tenets, many of which contributed to the development of AA's Twelve Steps.

- **Surrender:** The decision to submit one's will totally to God's will. Implied in the practice is the belief that God has a plan for one's life and one can seek His will and submit to or resist it. Surrender is a willful decision allowing God to direct every area of one's life.

- **Confession of Sin:** The Oxford Group understood sin to be "anything that keeps us from God or from one another."[4] Confessing one's sins to both God and another person was seen as essential for humility and communion with God.

- **Restitution:** Sin affects the lives of other people. The Oxford Group emphasized that righting the wrongs done to others was a vital ingredient in obedience to God.

- **Guidance:** God was understood to be personal and available. Oxford Groupers were encouraged to set aside time for daily prayer and meditation to seek God's face and receive direction and power for life.

- **Witnessing:** The Oxford Group embraced the belief that God uses people to affect the lives of others. A surrendered life enjoyed power and hope that all needed. Oxford Groupers were encouraged to share with others what God had done in their lives.

- **The Four Absolutes:** The example of Christ Himself was the standard of living in the Oxford Group. His example of holy living was held up as a banner by which Oxford Group members could measure their own behavior. Christ's life exemplified the Four Absolutes. These became guidelines for

---

3. Mel B., *New Wine* (Center City, Minn.: Hazelden, 1991), 33–34.
4. *What Is the Oxford Group?* (Center City, Minn.: Hazelden, 1933, 1997), 17.

behavior that Oxford Group members were challenged to apply daily in their lives.

1. Absolute Honesty
2. Absolute Purity
3. Absolute Unselfishness
4. Absolute Love

Dr. Bob and Bill were active members of the Oxford Group from 1935 until 1939. They went to meetings, practiced the Oxford Group principles, and intentionally sought to attract other alcoholics into the same life-changing relationship with God that they had experienced. They enjoyed significant success. About one hundred alcoholics found sobriety in the group through these two men's efforts.

In 1939 Bill and Bob, along with their followers, decided to split from the Oxford Group and created Alcoholics Anonymous. They changed more than their name. Fearful that religious ideas or jargon might repel prospective alcoholics, they intentionally purged all references to Christianity in their new program. AA's purpose, they reasoned, was sobriety, not salvation, so they wanted to make their program attractive and available to people of all faiths as well as to people with no faith. Consequently, when Oxford Group tenets were adapted into the Twelve Steps, the new group systematically removed references to Christ, sin, Holy Spirit, etc.

AA's Christian influence can still be detected with close inspection in the third edition of *Alcoholics Anonymous*. In the story "He Thought He Could Drink Like a Gentleman," we see Bill making an indirect reference to Christ. Bill and another member of AA, Clarence S., are attempting to help an active alcoholic get sober. The quote recalls the events from the perspective of the gentleman Bill and Clarence were attempting to help.

I do not recollect the specific conversation that went on but I believe I did challenge Bill to tell me something about A.A. and I do recall one other thing: I wanted to know *what this was that worked so many wonders,* and hanging over the mantel was *a picture of Gethsemane* and Bill pointed to it and said "There it is," which didn't make much sense to me.[5] (Italics added.)

Gethsemane was the garden that Christ prayed in just prior to His arrest and crucifixion. It was the place where Jesus again committed Himself to God's will, even at the expense of His own life. It was the place where Jesus prayed to God: "Yet not as I will, but as Thou wilt."

Other subtle references to AA's Christian roots can be found with further close inspection of AA's basic text, *Alcoholics Anonymous*. "Faith without works was dead" and "Thy will be done,"[6] both biblical concepts, are cornerstones of AA spirituality and alluded to in AA's basic text.

The Sermon on the Mount, the book of James, and the thirteenth chapter of 1 Corinthians were the spiritual cornerstones of many AA old-timers.[7] Some early members wanted AA to be called "The James Club" for their strong emphasis on the book of James.

---

5. *Alcoholics Anonymous*, 216–217.
6. Matt. 26:39
7. *'Pass It On': The Story of Bill Wilson and How the AA Message Reached the World* (New York: Alcoholics Anonymous World Services, 1984), 147.

AA is not a Christian program. But embedded in the Twelve Steps are spiritual principles that bring Christians into the thing that Frank Buchman intended—a dynamic relationship with Christ.

The balance of this book examines each Step from a biblical, Christian perspective. Every chapter lists AA's Step, a Christian adaptation of the Step, and the scriptural principle underlying it. All scriptural references are taken from the *New American Standard Bible,* unless otherwise noted.

To assist you in that goal of not just reading about the Steps but also applying them to your life, two types of worksheets are found in this book. One worksheet is designed for both individual and group discussion. If a Bible study, Sunday school class, or Twelve Step group wants to discuss the Christian principle in the Step, this worksheet can function as a helpful tool. It will look at the general principles and purpose of the Step and intentionally sidestep potentially embarrassing elements of sanctification that individuals might not want to discuss in a group setting. This worksheet, however, is not designed exclusively for group discussion. It can be completed individually by anyone who wants to grow spiritually.

The other type of worksheet is designed for individual reflection and application only. Each directs readers to look hard and honestly at their life and challenges them to change. Because the information in these worksheets is often personal, they are for each individual's eyes only, unless that person feels led to share the information with someone.

Most points developed in the following chapters have their root in Scripture. A list of Bible verses supporting the points made is also found in the back of each chapter. I encourage you to take time to reflect on these verses to deepen your understanding of the Christian disciplines they describe.

If you want to be close to Jesus, if you desire to do His will daily, if you want a sense of purpose and hope that comes with knowing and following Christ, read on.

CHAPTER FOUR

WEAKNESS: WE ARE POWERLESS TO LIVE THE CHRISTIAN LIFE

CHRISTIAN PRINCIPLE: WEAKNESS	AA'S STEP ONE	CHRISTIAN ADAPTATION
And He has said to me, "My grace is sufficient for you, for power is perfected in weakness." Most gladly, therefore, I will rather boast about my weaknesses, that the power of Christ may dwell in me. *2 Cor. 12:9* Apart from Me you can do nothing. *John 15:5*	We admitted we were powerless over alcohol—that our lives had become unmanageable.	We are powerless to live the Christian life.

John wasn't initially concerned despite facing a long prison sentence for drug trafficking. He confidently assumed that his drug money and high-priced lawyer would keep him from a severe punishment. Just in case his lawyer failed him, John decided to cover all the bases. He prayed a short, shallow, self-serving prayer: "God, please don't let me go to prison."

John quickly learned that his confidence was misplaced. The best deal his high-paid lawyer could bargain for was seven years in prison, far more than John was prepared to experience.

Now John was scared. His money had failed him, his lawyer had failed him—what was he to do? He appeared to run out of all resources except one: God. He now returned to God, but this time with a different attitude: one of des-

peration. Out of an abiding sense of powerlessness, John began to pray again, this time recognizing that God alone was his only hope.

What happened next was unexpected. While praying, John sensed an overwhelming presence of peace and love. It was so powerful that he wept uncontrollably in front of his cellmate, an out-of-character act for a street-hardened drug-trafficker. The next day, John was confronted by another inmate, a complete stranger, who claimed that God had directed him to let John know that "God loves you." These two elements propelled John into a new consciousness of God. He was no longer concerned about a long sentence because he was assured that God was with him.

John's experience reflects an essential key to a

relationship with Christ, the recognition of our dependence on Him, or our "weakness." John had always believed in and prayed to God, but his faith was truly in himself and his money. Until he was stripped of these false gods and realized his powerlessness, he could not experience the incredible benefit of a true relationship with Christ.

We too must understand our weakness to experience God's strength. Step One for Christians is the recognition of our state of utter weakness and dependence on God to accomplish His will in our lives.

God desires that our faith be in Him alone. Faith in our resources—money, intellect, education, power, or anything else—will prevent us from accessing God's power. Recognizing our "weakness" is essential to living out the Christian life because the life we are called to is humanly impossible to accomplish.

Genuine Christianity is the call to be like Christ. God desires His representatives to think like Him and to act like Him. His love must extend to others through us. His purity must be evident in our words and deeds. His holiness must be represented in our day-to-day experience. We desire to reflect His thoughts in our attitudes, to extend His mercy to those around us, and to duplicate His character in our daily affairs.

Yet this is humanly impossible. Christ's ideals are so incredibly high that they are unrealizable based solely on our desire to obey. Consider some of the things He commands us to do.

* Love your enemies and pray for those who persecute and mistreat you. (Matt. 5:44)
* Bless those who curse you. (Luke 6:28)
* Rejoice and be glad when you are persecuted for Christ's sake. (Matt. 5:11)
* Turn the other cheek when someone strikes you. (Luke 6:29)
* If someone steals your shirt, give him your coat. (Luke 6:29)
* Stop sinning. (1 John 2:1)

These standards are simply out of our reach; our corrupted human nature prohibits their attainment. Loving our enemies is about as easy for humans as flying by rapidly flapping our arms. Our impulse is to condemn, not forgive, to seek revenge, not mercy, to get and not give. Reflecting God's character is beyond our feeble human strength—we are powerless to do so because of our natural inclination to sin.

Many people hate the word *sin* because it suggests they are immoral or bad, and it causes feelings of shame. But to understand Christianity, to appreciate Christ, to live a Christian life, sin must be understood.

Sin is rebellion. It is the living out of attitudes and behaviors that are contrary to God's will. If God wants me to be sexually pure in my mind, yet I entertain sexual fantasies—this is sin. If God wants me to forgive my parents for a history of hurtful, abusive behavior, yet I don't—this is sin. If God wants me to be kind to my wife when I'm irritated by something she has done, yet I'm not kind—this is sin. If God wants me to be honest when completing my tax returns, yet I lie—this is sin. Any behavior or attitude that conflicts with God's will for me is sin.

Sin is instinctive. Today we often hear that humans are basically good. Poverty or some other unfortunate external influence is often blamed for immoral behavior. But the Christian view of human nature is different. We are born corrupt with an instinctive tendency to rebel—against authority and most important, against God.

Sin separates us from God. God, who is holy and sinless, cannot tolerate sin. He is light, and in Him is no darkness at all. Consequently our sinful tendencies place a humanly impenetrable wall between God and ourselves.

Overcoming sin is impossible with our own strength. We are powerless to undo sin's corrupting influence, to forgive ourselves, and to live the life God has called us to.

However, that which we are powerless to do, God has done for us through Christ. In His mercy God has forgiven our sins through the sacrificial death of His son, Jesus Christ. Through Christ, God has broken down the barrier that our sin has caused.

> While we were still helpless, at just the right time, Christ died for the ungodly. For one will hardly die for a righteous man; though perhaps for the good man someone would dare even to die. But God demonstrates his own love toward us, in that while we were yet sinners, Christ died for us.[1]

Christ's death has overcome sin in two ways. First, it has purchased mercy for us. God is now able to forgive us based on His son's sacrifice. The sin that separates us from God is washed away by Jesus' blood.

Second, Christ's death procured power for change. Our merciful God has called us to a life of purity and holiness that is to imitate Jesus. God would not challenge us to duplicate Christ's character unless we could do so. He would not call us to an impractical holiness or require that we forgive others if this were impossible.

All this is possible. Yet it comes through Christ alone—we are powerless to accomplish such a task. The ability to live out the Christian life and conform to His image comes exclusively from Him. He alone is able to transmit His character and love into our feeble human form. Christ loved—so can we. Christ forgave—so can we. Christ had self-control—so can we. Christ boldly proclaimed truth—so can we. Our willful determination to act like a Christian will have little effect without our desperate dependence on God to do so. Jesus rightly proclaims: "Apart from Me you can do nothing."[2]

The first-century church provides us a dynamic yet practical model for Christian living. The biblical examples of Peter, Stephen, or Paul illustrate what God can do through ordinary human beings who submit their will to Him. They strove to be like Christ, to duplicate His character in their day-to-day lives, and they succeeded.

Nothing has changed. Jesus continues to call His people into new lives that reflect His character. A friend of mind, Mary Jo, illustrates what Christ can do through us.

Mary Jo suffered an unimaginable loss: A drunk driver killed her son. The irony of this is that Mary Jo herself is a recovering alcoholic who after years of prayer, saw her son overcome his alcoholism. Now, a man driving in the wrong direction pointlessly ended her son's life. Her sober son driving in the right direction died; the drunk lived.

How would you respond if this had happened to you? Or perhaps a better question is: What would you like to see happen to your son's

---

1. Rom. 5:6–8
2. John 15:5

killer? My natural instinct would be for revenge. Somehow to make this person pay for the incredible pain I felt and loss I had experienced.

But Mary Jo, fueled by her relationship with Christ and her application of the Twelve Steps, did something different and remarkable: She asked for leniency for her son's killer. Instead of demanding the harshest punishment available, she asked the court to help her son's killer to be assessed for alcoholism and helped to change. In court she hugged him and told him she forgave him.

Is this response humanly possible? Is this something that you, I, or Mary Jo can do with our own power? Is this something we would even want to do? I believe the answer to all these questions is a resounding no! But with God's help, and our willingness to submit to His will, Christ Himself can provide us this type of character. Mary Jo's example of love and forgiveness demonstrates the power that God can provide those who earnestly seek Him.

WEAKNESS WORKSHEET
FOR GROUP DISCUSSION AND PERSONAL REFLECTION

This worksheet is designed for both personal reflection and group discussion. Do not rush through it. Prayerfully and thoughtfully consider how these verses apply to your life. Then in a small group, if possible, discuss each question.

1. **Based on the following scripture, where does sin come from?**

For from within, out of the heart of men, proceed the evil thoughts, fornications, thefts, murders, adulteries, deeds of coveting and wickedness, as well as deceit, sensuality, envy, slander, pride and foolishness. All these evil things proceed from within and defile the man.

Mark 7:21–23

2. **From God's perspective, what percentage of the population have sinned?**

Therefore, just as through one man sin entered into the world, and death through sin, and so death spread to all men, because all sinned.

Rom. 5:12

3. **What does this verse mean?**

For the wages of sin is death.

Rom. 6:23

4. **What does Paul mean when he suggests we were helpless? Also, what type of help did God provide us?**

For while we were still helpless, at the right time Christ died for the ungodly. For one will hardly die for a righteous man; though perhaps for the good man someone would dare even to die. But God demonstrates His own love toward us, in that while we were yet sinners, Christ died for us.

Rom. 5:6–8

5. **What is the outcome of our faith in Christ?**

There is therefore now no condemnation for those who are in Christ Jesus.

Rom. 8:1–4

6. Based on the following scriptures, as Christians, what are our standards of behavior and who is our example?

And every one who has this hope fixed on Him purifies himself, just as He is pure.

1 John 3:3

But like the Holy One who called you, be holy yourselves also in all your behavior; because it is written, "You shall be holy, for I am holy." *1 Pet. 1:15–16*

A pupil is not above his teacher; but everyone, after he has been fully trained, will be like his teacher. *Luke 6:40*

And be kind to one another, tender-hearted, forgiving each other, just as God in Christ also has forgiven you. Therefore be imitators of God, as beloved children; and walk in love, just as Christ also loved you, and gave Himself up for us, an offering and a sacrifice to God as a fragrant aroma. *Eph. 4:32–5:2*

7. **Based on the following scriptures, what are some of the attitudes and behaviors expected of Christians?**

Bless those who curse you, pray for those who mistreat you. Whoever hits you on the cheek, offer him the other also; and whoever takes away your coat, do not withhold your shirt from him either. *Luke 6:28–29*

But love your enemies, and do good, and lend, expecting nothing in return; and your reward will be great, and you will be sons of the Most High; for He Himself is kind to ungrateful and evil men. Be merciful, just as your Father is merciful. *Luke 6:35–36*

A new commandment I give to you, that you love one another, even as I have loved you, that you also love one another. *John 13:34*

No one who is born of God practices sin, because His seed abides in him; and he cannot sin, because he is born of God. *1 John 3:9*

8. Based on the following scriptures, what is our only source of power to live out the Christian life?

I am the vine, you are the branches; he who abides in Me, and I in him, he bears much fruit; for apart from Me you can do nothing.   *John 15:5*

And to know the love of Christ which surpasses knowledge, that you may be filled up to all the fullness of God. Now to Him who is able to do exceeding abundantly beyond all that we ask or think, according to the power that works within us . . .
                                                                                        Eph. 3:19–20

Brethren, my heart's desire and my prayer to God for them is for their salvation. For I bear them witness that they have a zeal for God, but not in accordance with knowledge. For not knowing about God's righteousness, and seeking to establish their own, they did not subject themselves to the righteousness of God. For Christ is the end of the law for righteousness to everyone who believes.

Rom. 10:1–4

1. What does Paul mean when he states they sought to establish a righteousness of their own?

2. In Paul's time, circumcision was mistakenly thought to establish righteousness. What religious or nonreligious rituals today do people use to establish their own righteousness?

3. Based on the above passage, what is the righteousness that God approves of?

4. Have you trusted in the participation of religious rituals to establish righteousness? If so, which ones?

5. Based on the following scripture, what is God's basis for our forgiveness?

For by grace you have been saved through faith; and that not of yourselves, it is the gift of God; not as a result of works, that no one should boast. For we are His workmanship, created in Christ Jesus for good works, which God prepared beforehand, that we should walk in them.

Eph. 2:8–10

SCRIPTURES RELATED TO WEAKNESS

ALL HAVE SINNED

For all of us have become like one who is unclean, And all our righteous deeds are like a filthy garment; And all of us wither like a leaf, And our iniquities, like the wind, take us away. *Is. 64:6*

For all have sinned and fall short of the glory of God. *Rom. 3:23*

Therefore, just as through one man sin entered into the world, and death through sin, and so death spread to all men, because all sinned. *Rom. 5:12*

If we say that we have no sin, we are deceiving ourselves, and the truth is not in us. If we confess our sins, He is faithful and righteous to forgive us our sins and to cleanse us from all unrighteousness. If we say that we have not sinned, we make Him a liar, and His word is not in us. *1 John 1:8–10*

WAGES OF SIN—DEATH

For the wages of sin is death, but the free gift of God is eternal life in Christ Jesus our Lord. *Rom. 6:23*

Now the deeds of the flesh are evident, which are: immorality, impurity, sensuality, idolatry, sorcery, enmities, strife, jealousy, outbursts of anger, disputes, dissensions, factions, envyings, drunkenness, carousings, and things like these, of which I forewarn you just as I have forewarned you that those who practice such things shall not inherit the kingdom of God. *Gal. 5:19–21*

And you were dead in your trespasses and sins, in which you formerly walked according to the course of this world, according to the prince of the power of the air, of the spirit that is now working in the sons of disobedience. Among them we too all formerly lived in the lusts of our flesh, indulging the desires of the flesh and of the mind, and were by nature children of wrath, even as the rest. *Eph. 2:1–5*

And when you were dead in your transgressions and the uncircumcision of your flesh, He made you alive together with Him, having forgiven us all our transgressions. *Col. 2:13*

THE SOURCE OF SIN—THE HEART

For out of the heart come evil thoughts, murders, adulteries, fornications, thefts, false witness, slanders. *Matt. 15:19*

For from within, out of the heart of men, proceed the evil thoughts, fornications, thefts, murders, adulteries, deeds of coveting and wickedness, as well as deceit, sensuality, envy, slander, pride and foolishness. All these evil things proceed from within and defile the man. *Mark 7:21–23*

CHRIST'S POWER—FORGIVENESS OF SIN

For while we were still helpless, at the right time Christ died for the ungodly. *Rom. 5:6*

In Him we have redemption through His blood, the forgiveness of our trespasses, according to the riches of His grace. *Eph. 1:7*

And be kind to one another, tender-hearted, forgiving each other, just as God in Christ also has forgiven you. *Eph. 4:32*

But God, being rich in mercy, because of His great love with which He loved us, even when we were dead in our transgressions, made us alive together with Christ (by grace you have been saved). *Eph. 2:4–5*

For we also once were foolish ourselves, disobedient, deceived, enslaved to various lusts and pleasures, spending our life in malice and envy, hateful, hating one another. But when the kindness of God our Savior and His love for mankind appeared, He saved us, not on the basis of deeds which we have done in righteousness, but according to His mercy, by the washing of regeneration and renewing by the Holy Spirit. *Titus 3:3–5*

CHRISTIANS—CALLED TO BE LIKE CHRIST

You have heard that it was said, "You shall love your neighbor, and hate your enemy." But I say to you, love your enemies, and pray for those who persecute you in order that you may be sons of your Father who is in heaven; for He causes His sun to rise on the evil and the good, and sends rain on the righteous and the unrighteous. For if you love those who love you, what reward have you? Do not even the tax-gatherers do the same? And if you greet your brothers only, what do you do more than others? Do not even the Gentiles do the same? Therefore you are to be perfect, as your heavenly Father is perfect. *Matt. 5:43–48*

But love your enemies, and do good, and lend, expecting nothing in return; and your reward will be great, and you will be sons of the Most High; for He Himself is kind to ungrateful and evil men. Be merciful, just as your Father is merciful. *Luke 6:35–36*

A pupil is not above his teacher; but everyone, after he has been fully trained, will be like his teacher. *Luke 6:40*

A new commandment I give to you, that you love one another, even as I have loved you, that you also love one another. *John 13:34*

This is My commandment, that you love one another, just as I have loved you. *John 15:12*

Be imitators of me, just as I also am of Christ. *1 Cor. 11:1*

And be kind to one another, tender-hearted, forgiving each other, just as God in Christ also has forgiven you. Therefore be imitators of God, as beloved children; and walk in love, just as Christ also loved you, and gave Himself up for us, an offering and a sacrifice to God as a fragrant aroma. *Eph. 4:32–5:2*

But like the Holy One who called you, be holy yourselves also in all your behavior; because it is written, "You shall be holy, for I am holy." *1 Pet. 1:15–16*

And every one who has this hope fixed on Him purifies himself, just as He is pure. *1 John 3:3*

CHRIST'S POWER—
LIVING THE CHRISTIAN LIFE

I am the vine, you are the branches; he who abides in Me, and I in him, he bears much fruit; for apart from Me you can do nothing.

John 15:5

And to know the love of Christ which surpasses knowledge, that you may be filled up to all the fullness of God. Now to Him who is able to do exceeding abundantly beyond all that we ask or think, according to the power that works within us . . .

Eph. 3:19–20

For if you are living according to the flesh, you must die; but if by the Spirit you are putting to death the deeds of the body, you will live. For all who are being led by the Spirit of God, these are sons of God.

Rom. 8:13–14

But I say, walk by the Spirit, and you will not carry out the desire of the flesh. For the flesh sets its desire against the Spirit, and the Spirit against the flesh; for these are in opposition to one another, so that you may not do the things that you please. But if you are led by the Spirit, you are not under the Law. Now the deeds of the flesh are evident, which are: immorality, impurity, sensuality, idolatry, sorcery, enmities, strife, jealousy, outbursts of anger, disputes, dissensions, factions, envyings, drunkenness, carousings, and things like these, of which I forewarn you just as I have forewarned you that those who practice such things shall not inherit the kingdom of God. But the fruit of the Spirit is love, joy, peace, patience, kindness, goodness, faithfulness, gentleness, self-control; against such things there is no law. Now those who belong to Christ Jesus have crucified the flesh with its passions and desires. If we live by the Spirit, let us also walk by the Spirit.

Gal. 5:16–25

CHAPTER FIVE

EXPERIENCING CHRIST:
JESUS IS ALIVE AND AVAILABLE

CHRISTIAN PRINCIPLE: JESUS IS ALIVE AND AVAILABLE	AA'S STEP TWO	CHRISTIAN ADAPTATION
Come to Me, all who are weary and heavy-laden, and I will give you rest. *Matt. 11:28* I am with you always, even to the end of the age. *Matt. 28:20*	Came to believe that a Power greater than ourselves could restore us to sanity.	To experience Jesus as personal and available.

For years I have studied the career of Minnesota Vikings receiver Cris Carter. I read newspapers, listened to sports experts evaluate his ability, and frequently watched him perform at an amazing level of skill. My observations convinced me that he is one of the best receivers ever to play professional football.

My son and I were invited to a breakfast where Carter was speaking. He sat at our table, looked into our eyes, shook our hands, and answered our questions about professional football and his life.

This meeting dramatically changed my knowledge of Carter. He was no longer a sports figure being studied from a distance, but a real person. A person not just capable of making amazing catches but also of having personal contact with others.

Many Christians mistakenly presume that a belief in God is identical to experiencing Christ. Yet all too often, Christian faith is built on ideas only—not a relationship with Christ Himself.

Billions of people know about Jesus. They have been taught that He exists, that He died for our sins and was resurrected. They proudly participate in church or check the "Christian" box when filling out a questionnaire inquiring about their religious affiliation. But they don't know Him or hear His voice, and they can't truly follow Him because they lack a personal relationship with Him.

Religious activities and adherence to church doctrines are no substitute for Christ's personal communion in our lives. Genuine Christianity demands that we have a person-to-person relationship with Jesus, a relationship that transcends mere ideas. We must experience Christ as available, personal, loving, and intimate. We must know that He cares for us and desires a relationship with us, that He is willing and able to forgive us, love us, and assist us in our day-to-day lives. We must feel that He is able to give us the strength to manage all the challenges that life pitches our way.

A mere intellectual belief system is inadequate for such a task. Imagine a pilot of a jumbo jet approaching a landing in a crowded metropolitan airport. As the pilot guides the plane toward the landing strip, the copilot becomes concerned because the pilot has had *no contact at all* with the control tower, and the copilot sees another plane coming toward them. He hurriedly asks, "Aren't you going to confirm with the control tower clearance for our approach?" "No," the pilot confidently asserts. "It's okay because I believe in the control tower, that's enough for me." How would you like to be on that jet? Believing in a control tower is no substitute for communication with it—and believing in God is no substitute for communing with Him.

I first experienced God in New York City. On December 5, 1979, I checked into the Smithers Treatment Center on East Ninety-third Street in Manhattan. Smithers was an impressive mansion, previously owned by a famous theater producer, Billy Rose. Now, instead of entertaining famous actors and actresses, it housed about thirty addicts; some just killing time, others desperate not to die.

Once admitted, I breathed a great sigh of relief. "Finally," I thought I was safe. Here, in the protection of this program, I hoped to find the strength and support required to reverse my life's misfortunes.

Smithers taught AA's Twelve Steps as a resource for abstinence. These Steps, however, did not line up with my arrogant way of thinking. They presumed that God's assistance was both available and necessary to experience recovery. I was perfectly willing to sober up, but to be brainwashed into a false belief system seemed cruel, unreasonable, and unnecessary. My warped thinking confidently assured me that God couldn't exist because I never saw a hint of Him: no burning bush, no audible voice—nothing. So why should I presume He exists simply because some ex-drunks tell me so? It just didn't make any sense to me at the time, but that was soon to change.

Day two in treatment presented a deadly threat—I wanted to leave. I was reaping the unpleasant consequences of years of daily heavy drug and alcohol use—severe physical withdrawal. I couldn't sleep, I was agitated, I felt sick, and I desperately wanted to feel better.

Leaving treatment and getting high could ensure immediate relief, but this was not a great plan. I knew that if I chose that path, I would be diving headlong into the depressive hopelessness that had led me to treatment. What was I to do? I knew I needed to stay, but a powerful force was drawing me away. Like the man whom the river current dragged to the edge of a huge waterfall, destined to land on the rocks below, I felt powerless to prevent my next self-destructive act.

In this desperate state an unlikely yet important idea occurred to me: "What about God? Perhaps the God of AA can help me with this dilemma. These so-called experts suggest that God exists, that He can help; perhaps I should find out for myself if He is real, available, and able to help me. So I prayed my first prayer:

"God if you truly exist—reveal yourself to me in a way that I can understand."

What happened next was completely unexpected. Within moments of that prayer I sensed a warm, soothing, and tangible presence surround me. Like a freezing man entering a warm bath I felt completely engulfed by comforting warmth. As loving parents nurture their desperately ill child, God reassured me of His reality with His comforting embrace.

This life-changing experience continued for hours into the evening and radically transformed my conceptions about God. I could doubt no longer. The atheistic cynicism immediately melted away and in its place came the astounding insight—God is real!

I now understood God's mercy. My addictions, atheism, and arrogant selfishness were not barriers to Jesus. My sin was no match for His forgiveness. My hate was no match for His love. My self-righteous arrogance was no match for His life-giving mercy.

My impulse to leave treatment was replaced with a renewed desire to complete what I had begun, or perhaps what God had begun. My obsession to relapse was lifted, and in its place burned a bright hope of the future. The power required to complete treatment and stay chemical-free was a gracious gift that accompanied this experience. That evening, in a large, dark bedroom in a Manhattan mansion, I "came to believe" that God was real and cared about me as an individual.

The Bible gives us many examples of people who experience a life-changing relationship with Jesus. Perhaps the most powerful of all is the experience of Saul of Tarsus, who became the Apostle Paul.

Prior to his conversion, Saul believed in God but lacked a personal relationship with Him. He prayed to God but didn't know Him. He went to temple, but didn't hear Him. Saul followed the customs of his religion but didn't follow God. Saul's misguided understanding of God's will in his life actually led him to become an enemy of God despite his apparent reverence for Him.

The preconversion Saul viewed Jesus as a deceased troublemaker, a false prophet whose dangerous teachings were being furthered by his disciples. It never occurred to Saul that Jesus was in fact who He claimed to be—the Son of God who had died for all and was now living in and through them who are His. No, in Saul's mind Jesus was dead, completely dead. He had been publicly crucified, buried, and was never to be seen again.

But Jesus was alive, and He was about to reveal Himself to Saul in a dramatic and powerful way. In a blinding, flashing light on the road to Damascus, Jesus spoke to Saul and asked, "Why do you persecute Me?"[1] When Saul inquired of this bodiless voice "Who are you Lord?" he received the shock of his life when Christ responded, "I am Jesus whom you are persecuting."[2]

Saul learned through experience what all Christians must learn—that Jesus is alive. He is risen from the dead through the mighty power of His Heavenly Father. And though He no longer walks the earth, He continues to reveal

---

1. Acts 9:4
2. Acts 9:5

Himself to people as vital, alive, available.

Jesus called Saul by name, exposed his sin, and then called him into a relationship despite his lifestyle. Jesus is not an impersonal force who has no interest in people. He is intimately aware of and concerned about us as individuals. He knows our names and deeds, and He desires an intimate relationship with us despite what we've done.

Jesus forgave the repentant Saul and in so doing created within Saul an intense desire to serve. Saul dedicated the rest of his life to Christian ministry. Later, Saul described Christ's purpose in forgiving him.

> It is a trustworthy statement, deserving full acceptance, that Christ Jesus came into the world to save sinners, among whom I am foremost of all. And yet for this reason I found mercy, in order that in me as the foremost, Jesus Christ might demonstrate His perfect patience, as an example for those who would believe in Him for eternal life.[3]

Saul's sin could not overcome Christ's mercy. He proclaims, "If Christ can forgive me after what I have done, He can forgive anyone."

We may not share Saul's sin, yet we have all sinned and fallen short of God's standards.

Through Saul's example God wants us to experience His forgiving Love. No matter what we have done, no matter how we have sinned, no matter whom we have hurt, God desires a relationship with us. Through Christ He is able to forgive, accept, and love us. He can and will restore us if we, like Saul, turn to Him, receive His mercy, and seek His will.

Jesus desires that we experience His love personally. He must not be simply known about—He must be known. He must not be only related to—He must be related with. Jesus is not indifferent or uncaring; He is not aloof or unavailable. He is our divine brother who seeks to guide, nurture, direct, and strengthen us in life's challenges and joys.

Seeking is the key to experiencing God: He assures us that if we seek Him we shall find Him.[4] Our determined and desperate desire to know Him will provide us access to His love and will. As we seek God, He will reveal Himself to us in a way that enables us to come to believe. Just as scales fell from Saul's eyes when Barnabus confirmed Christ's reality to Saul, so, too, God will remove the spiritual blindness from our hearts and allow us truly to know Him as we fervently seek His face.

---

3. 1 Tim.: 15–16
4. Deut. 4:29, Prov. 8:17, Jer. 29:13

EXPERIENCING WORKSHEET
FOR GROUP DISCUSSION AND PERSONAL REFLECTION

1. Have you ever experienced Christ in a personal way? If so, how and when?

2. Acts 9:1–18 describes the conversion of Saul of Tarsus. Read these verses, then answer the following questions.

Who initiated the first contact, Saul or Jesus? (See also Luke 19:10.)

After his blinding light experience, what did Saul do to seek Christ further?

How did Jesus respond to Saul's efforts to seek Him?

Based on Saul's experience, what are some of the key elements of experiencing Jesus?

3. Based on the below verses, what are some of the circumstances that allow us to experience Christ?

For where two or three have gathered together in My name, there I am in their midst.

Matt. 18:20

Blessed are those who hunger and thirst for righteousness, for they shall be satisfied.

Matt. 5:6

I will not leave you as orphans; I will come to you. After a little while the world will behold Me no more; but you will behold Me; because I live, you shall live also. In that day you shall know that I am in My Father, and you in Me, and I in you. He who has My commandments and keeps them, he it is who loves Me; and he who loves Me shall be loved by My Father, and I will love him, and will disclose Myself to him.

John 14:18–21

4. Numerous scriptures make clear that our experience of Jesus will be the result of earnestly seeking Him. Consider the verses below and list ways you have already sought God and ways you can continue to seek Him.

But from there you will seek the Lord your God, and you will find Him if you search for Him with all your heart and all your soul.

Deut. 4:29

I love those who love me; And those who diligently seek me will find me.

Prov. 8:17

And you will seek Me and find Me, when you search for Me with all your heart.

Jer. 29:13

SCRIPTURES RELATED TO WEAKNESS

Jesus Is Alive

"Behold, the virgin shall be with child, and shall bear a Son, and they shall call His name Immanuel," which translated means, "God with us." *Matt. 1:23*

For where two or three have gathered together in My name, there I am in their midst. *Matt. 18:20*

I will not leave you as orphans; I will come to you. After a little while the world will behold Me no more; but you will behold Me; because I live, you shall live also. *John 14:18–19*

And the Lord said to Paul in the night by a vision, "Do not be afraid any longer, but go on speaking and do not be silent; for I am with you, and no man will attack you in order to harm you, for I have many people in this city." *Acts 18:9–10*

But the Lord stood with me, and strengthened me, in order that through me the proclamation might be fully accomplished, and that all the Gentiles might hear; and I was delivered out of the lion's mouth. *2 Tim. 4:17*

He Is Personal: Jesus Is Our Friend and Brother, God Is Our Father

For whoever shall do the will of My Father who is in heaven, he is My brother and sister and mother. *Matt. 12:50*

And the King will answer and say to them, Truly I say to you, to the extent that you did it to one of these brothers of Mine, even the least of them, you did it to Me. *Matt. 25:40*

You are My friends, if you do what I command you. No longer do I call you slaves; for the slave does not know what his master is doing; but I have called you friends, for all things that I have heard from My Father I have made known to you. *John 15:14–15*

Jesus said to her, "Stop clinging to Me; for I have not yet ascended to the Father; but go to My brethren, and say to them, 'I ascend to My Father and your Father, and My God and your God.'" *John 20:17*

For whom He foreknew, He also predestined to become conformed to the image of His Son, that He might be the first-born among many brethren. *Rom. 8:29*

And because you are sons, God has sent forth the Spirit of His Son into our hearts, crying, "Abba! Father!" *Gal. 4:6*

And the Scripture was fulfilled which says, "And Abraham believed God, and it was reckoned to him as righteousness," and he was called the friend of God. *James 2:23*

He Is Merciful

Seek the Lord while He may be found; Call upon Him while He is near. Let the wicked forsake his way, and the unrighteous man his thoughts; and let him return to the Lord, and He will have compassion on him; and to our God, For He will abundantly pardon. "For My thoughts are not your thoughts, Neither are your ways My ways," declares the Lord. *Is. 55:6–8*

And this is the very thing I wrote you, lest, when I came, I should have sorrow from those who ought to make me rejoice; having confidence in you all, that my joy would be the joy of you all.

2 Cor. 2:3

But God, being rich in mercy, because of His great love with which He loved us . . .   *Eph. 2:4*

Blessed be the God and Father of our Lord Jesus Christ, who according to His great mercy has caused us to be born again to a living hope through the resurrection of Jesus Christ from the dead.   *1 Pet. 1:3*

He Is Practical: He Is Able and Willing to Meet Our Needs

For the Lord God is a sun and shield; The Lord gives grace and glory; No good thing does He withhold from those who walk uprightly.

Ps. 84:11

For all these things the nations of the world eagerly seek; but your Father knows that you need these things. But seek for His kingdom, and these things shall be added to you. Do not be afraid, little flock, for your Father has chosen gladly to give you the kingdom. Sell your possessions and give to charity; make yourselves purses which do not wear out, an unfailing treasure in heaven, where no thief comes near, nor moth destroys.   *Luke 12:30–33*

And my God shall supply all your needs according to His riches in glory in Christ Jesus.

Phil. 4:19

Let your way of life be free from the love of money, being content with what you have; for He Himself has said, "I will never desert you, nor will I ever forsake you."   *Heb. 13:5*

He Must Be Sought to Be Found

But from there you will seek the Lord your God, and you will find Him if you search for Him with all your heart and all your soul.

Deut. 4:29

As for you, my son Solomon, know the God of your father, and serve Him with a whole heart and a willing mind; for the Lord searches all hearts, and understands every intent of the thoughts. If you seek Him, He will let you find Him; but if you forsake Him, He will reject you forever.   *1 Chron. 28:9*

I love those who love me; And those who diligently seek me will find me.   *Prov. 8:17*

And you will seek Me and find Me, when you search for Me with all your heart.   *Jer. 29:13*

Ask, and it shall be given to you; seek, and you shall find; knock, and it shall be opened to you. For every one who asks receives, and he who seeks finds, and to him who knocks it shall be opened.   *Matt. 7:7–8*

And without faith it is impossible to please Him, for he who comes to God must believe that He is, and that He is a rewarder of those who seek Him.   *Heb. 11:6*

CHAPTER SIX

REPENTANCE: COMPLETELY SURRENDER OUR LIFE TO CHRIST

CHRISTIAN PRINCIPLE: REPENTANCE	AA'S STEP THREE	CHRISTIAN ADAPTATION
If anyone wishes to come after Me, let him deny himself, and take up his cross daily, and follow Me. *Luke 9:23*	Made a decision to turn our will and our lives over to the care of God *as we understood Him.*	We decided to *completely* surrender our lives over to Jesus.

My years of skepticism about chiropractors was tested when my lower back developed an unpleasant chronic pain. Reluctantly I made an appointment, was examined, and received a course of treatment.

At first I resisted the recommended treatment. The recommendations would take time and cost money, and I wasn't convinced of their value.

My resistance to treatment didn't help my back. The pain continued and eventually provided me with a new level of willingness to submit to my chiropractor's recommendation. When I finally did as I was told, my back pain entirely disappeared.

Experiencing Christ in our lives is no guarantee we will submit to His will and purpose. Just as I can seek a doctor's advice and ignore the prescribed treatment, so I can experience Jesus

in my life and ignore His directions. Once we experience Christ in a personal way, we are confronted with a critical question: Whom will I serve—Jesus or myself?

Biblical Christianity is radical. It demands a lifestyle that is contrary to our natural impulses and at odds with the culture at large. To comply with the words, directives, and commands of Jesus requires a willingness to change at every level of our lives. The decision to turn from our ways and replace them with God's ways is called repentance.

Repentance is the decision to turn away from our life plans to God's plan. The decision to repent affects every area of our lives—what we say, think, and do and how we do it.

The Bible records that Jesus, as well as His disciples, called all people to repent. Repentance was proclaimed to the rich as well as the poor, to the religious as well as the irreligious. From His perspective all had sinned and were being challenged to repent.[1]

The challenge of repentance continues to this day. Jesus asks each of us to choose whom we will serve—Him or ourselves. His desire is that we willingly surrender all that we hold dear and replace it with God's purposes and designs for our life. This means that everything we love is up for grabs. All our ambitions and desires become willingly subject to whatever changes He has designed for us.

Jesus practiced what He preached. His life was a perfect illustration of complete submission to His Heavenly Father. The Bible records that on numerous occasions Jesus sought His Heavenly Father's will and submitted to it, even at the cost of His comfort, His dignity, and His life. Jesus said:

> For I have come down from heaven, not to do My own will, but the will of Him who sent Me.[2]

Also, when contemplating his imminent crucifixion, Jesus said:

> Father, if Thou art willing, remove this cup from Me; yet not My will, but Thine be done.[3]

Jesus' words, His life, and His death provide for us a powerful example of submission, placing first and foremost the will of His Heavenly Father. This is the same attitude that God desires for us.

True repentance demands a lifelong commitment. Claiming discipleship without being fully prepared to live out God's plan for our entire life is a serious mistake. Jesus warns his followers to count the costs before making this decision. Counting the costs involves recognizing that God is calling us to a lifetime of service that will demand many sacrifices.

Are we willing to make such a commitment, or will we profess a faith that lacks obedience and consequently be another example of Christian hypocrisy? Jesus challenges us to consider carefully what we are committing ourselves to. Clearly, His preference is that we are prepared whole-heartedly to follow through with this decision to follow Him.[4]

So what might the cost of discipleship be for you? What might God desire to change in your life? Could He ask you to change jobs, friends, or hobbies? Might He require that you move to a different community? Might He ask you to become a missionary or serve meals to the homeless or give all your money to the poor? Might He ask that you share your faith with people who aren't interested? Might He ask you to say and do things that result in others' ridicule and judgment of you as a religious fanatic? If He does require these changes, are you willing to change? Are you willing to let God reign completely in your life no matter what He desires for you? Though God's future plan for us

---

1. See verses at the end of the chapter.
2. John 6:38
3. Luke 22:42
4. Luke 14:25–35

may be unclear, He requires advance willingness on our part to obey.

As we consider the costs of true discipleship, we can be confident of one thing—God desires our sanctification. Sanctification is the process by which our thoughts and actions become more and more like God's so that we might be effective in His service. His views become ours, His Love becomes ours, His thoughts become ours. We need not be confused about this. God wants His children to be pure, walk in holiness, and conform to the image of His Son Jesus. A genuine follower of Christ will seek to be rid of attitudes and behaviors that are sinful.

Self-denial is actually great gain. By losing our lives we are not giving up anything of real value. God loves us, and any change He directs us to will always be beneficial. Whatever sacrifices He requires from us are for our good. They enable us to experience the incredible benefits of an intimate relationship with Him. Our life, without Christ, is heavy and burdensome, but Christ's yoke is easy and light. He promises always to be with us, to provide us strength in our weakness, to ensure that our basic needs are met, and to give us hope in hopeless situations. No personal sacrifice outweighs the incredible benefits that a repentant lifestyle provides. If we lose our empty and purposeless life for His sake, we truly find life. Consider Christ's words to Peter who desired to know the benefit of a life devoted to Christ.

And Peter said, "Behold, we have left our own homes, and followed You." And He said to them, "Truly I say to you, there is no one who has left house or wife or brothers or parents or children, for the sake of the kingdom of God, who shall not receive many times as much at this time and in the age to come, eternal life."[5]

So God asks you to decide: Are you content to pursue your life, or His? Are you willing to lose your life no matter the personal sacrifices? Are you willing to change behaviors, jobs, friends, or attitudes if God desires you to change? Do you trust that God's will for your life is superior to your own, and do you earnestly desire to complete His purpose for you? Are you anxious to see how God can and will use your failures for His successes? If you answer yes, then you are ready to lose your life.

If fear or distrust is preventing your complete surrender—pray. Ask God to help you to experience Him in a way that will assure you that His plan is best. Let Christ know in your own words your desire to surrender your life to Him.

Repentance is just a beginning. It opens the door to the intimacy that God desires for us and that we were created for. Now with God's help, we must strive to become the person God desires.

---

5. Luke 18:28–30

REPENTANCE WORKSHEET
FOR GROUP DISCUSSION AND PERSONAL REFLECTION

1. **Read Luke 18:18–30, and then discuss the following questions.**

What stood in the way of the ruler's relationship with God?

Based on this barrier, what was Jesus' suggested remedy?

Why did the ruler resist taking Jesus' advice?

Other than money, what are other barriers to living out the Christian faith?

Based on what Jesus told both the ruler and his disciples, what are the benefits of making personal sacrifices in our relationship with God?

2. **Read Luke 14:25-35, and then answer the following questions.**

What level of commitment does Jesus desire of His disciple?

What does Jesus mean by "counting the costs" before becoming a disciple?

Why is it important that we count the costs before committing our lives to Christ? (See also Matt. 13:21.)

REPENTANCE WORKSHEETS
FOR PERSONAL REFLECTION ONLY

The following exercise is designed to have you consider what you presently hold dear and to evaluate your willingness to surrender these key areas of your life to God.

Your life need not be perfectly in line with God's will to make this commitment. All that's required of you is the willingness to change. If you currently have that willingness, let God know in your own words that you will follow Him no matter the cost or changes He desires of you.

If you find yourself ambivalent or uncertain of your level of commitment, ask God to help you become more willing. Ask that He help you remove any trace of resistance toward His design for your life.

KEY AREA OF LIFE: MONEY

Describe your current attitude toward money. Is it very important? Do you derive security from it?	
What is your current practice with money? Saving? Spending? Hoarding? Self-indulgence?	
Do you believe that your current practice and attitude toward money are consistent with God's will? Yes. No. Not sure. If you answered no or not sure, please describe why.	
If God required you to change your practice and attitude toward money, would you be willing?	

KEY AREA OF LIFE: POSSESSIONS

List the material possessions that you value most. Car? Home? Stereo? Computer? Clothing? Cosmetics? Boat? Motorcycle? etc.	
What is your current attitude toward material possessions? How important are they to you?	
Do any of the above possessions compete with God for your affection?	
Do you believe that your current practice and attitude toward possessions are consistent with God's will? Yes. No. Not sure. If you answered no or not sure, please describe why.	
If God required you to change your practice and attitude toward some or all of your material possessions, would you be willing?	

KEY AREA OF LIFE: SEX

Describe your current practice of sex. Never? Frequent? Always with spouse? Extramarital? Premarital? etc.	
What is your current attitude toward sex? Is it important? Are you preoccupied with it?	
Do you believe that your current practice and attitude toward sex are consistent with God's will? Yes. No. Not sure. If you answered no or not sure, please describe why.	
If God required you to change your practice and attitude toward sex, would you be willing?	

KEY AREA OF LIFE: RELATIONSHIP WITH FAMILY

Describe your relationships with key family members: spouse, children, parents, etc. Are they loving, distant, resentful, abusive, etc.? (Use extra paper if needed.)	
Do you believe that your current relationship with these family members is consistent with God's will? Yes. No. Not sure. If you answered no or not sure, please describe why.	
If God required you to change your practice and attitude toward some family members, would you be willing?	

KEY AREA OF LIFE: RELATIONSHIP WITH FRIENDS AND ASSOCIATES	
Describe your relationships with key friends and associates. Who are they? What is the nature of these relationships?	
Do you believe that your current relationship with these people is consistent with God's will? Yes. No. Not sure. If you answered no or not sure, please describe why.	
If God required you to change your practice and attitude toward some or all of these relationships, would you be willing?	

KEY AREA OF LIFE: VOCATION OR CAREER

Describe your vocation or career: homemaker, butcher, business owner, etc.	
Do you believe that your current vocation is consistent with God's will? Yes. No. Not sure. If you answered no or not sure, please describe why.	
Do you believe that your current attitude or practice of your vocation is consistent with God's will? Yes. No. Not sure. If you answered no or not sure, please describe why.	
If God required you to change your job or your attitude and practice of your vocation, would you be willing?	

KEY AREA OF LIFE: RECREATION AND ENTERTAINMENT

Describe your current sources of entertainment and recreation. TV? Movies? Sports? Boating? Reading? Shopping? etc.	
Do you believe that your current practice and attitude toward recreation and entertainment are consistent with God's will? Yes. No. Not sure. If you answered no or not sure, please describe why.	
If God required you to change your practice and attitude toward recreation and entertainment, would you be willing?	

KEY AREA OF LIFE: SINFUL HABITS	
What, if any, habits do you have that may be inconsistent with God's purpose for you?: Gambling? Overeating? Cursing? etc.	
If God required you to change or completely eliminate certain habits, would you be willing to?	

SCRIPTURES RELATED TO REPENTANCE

WE ALL MUST REPENT

. . . saying, "The time is fulfilled, and the kingdom of God is at hand; repent and believe in the gospel."   *Mark 1:15*

I have not come to call righteous men but sinners to repentance.   *Luke 5:32*

I tell you, no, but unless you repent, you will all likewise perish.   *Luke 13:5*

I tell you that in the same way, there will be more joy in heaven over one sinner who repents, than over ninety-nine righteous persons who need no repentance.   *Luke 15:7*

In the same way, I tell you, there is joy in the presence of the angels of God over one sinner who repents.   *Luke 15:10*

But he said, "No, Father Abraham, but if someone goes to them from the dead, they will repent!"   *Luke 16:30*

Be on your guard! If your brother sins, rebuke him; and if he repents, forgive him. And if he sins against you seven times a day, and returns to you seven times, saying, "I repent," forgive him.   *Luke 17:3–4*

. . . that repentance for forgiveness of sins should be proclaimed in His name to all the nations, beginning from Jerusalem.   *Luke 24:47*

And Peter said to them, "Repent, and let each of you be baptized in the name of Jesus Christ for the forgiveness of your sins; and you shall receive the gift of the Holy Spirit."   *Acts 2:38*

Repent therefore and return, that your sins may be wiped away, in order that times of refreshing may come from the presence of the Lord.
                                    Acts 3:19

Therefore repent of this wickedness of yours, and pray the Lord that if possible, the intention of your heart may be forgiven you.   *Acts 8:22*

Therefore having overlooked the times of ignorance, God is now declaring to men that all everywhere should repent.   *Acts 17:30*

And Paul said, "John baptized with the baptism of repentance, telling the people to believe in Him who was coming after him, that is, in Jesus."   *Acts 19:4*

Remember therefore from where you have fallen, and repent and do the deeds you did at first; or else I am coming to you, and will remove your lampstand out of its place—unless you repent.   *Rev. 2:5*

Repent therefore; or else I am coming to you quickly, and I will make war against them with the sword of My mouth.   *Rev. 2:16*

And I gave her time to repent; and she does not want to repent of her immorality. Behold, I will cast her upon a bed of sickness, and those who commit adultery with her into great tribulation, unless they repent of her deeds.   *Rev. 2:21–22*

Remember therefore what you have received and heard; and keep it, and repent. If therefore you will not wake up, I will come like a thief, and you will not know at what hour I will come upon you.   *Rev. 3:3*

Those whom I love, I reprove and discipline; be zealous therefore, and repent.   *Rev. 3:19*

JESUS ALWAYS SUBMITTED TO HIS HEAVENLY FATHER'S WILL

Father, if Thou art willing, remove this cup from Me; yet not My will, but Thine be done.
                                                    Luke 22:42

Jesus said to them, "My food is to do the will of Him who sent Me, and to accomplish His work."
                                                    John 4:34

I can do nothing on My own initiative. As I hear, I judge; and My judgment is just, because I do not seek My own will, but the will of Him who sent Me.   *John 5:30*

For I have come down from heaven, not to do My own will, but the will of Him who sent Me.
                                                    John 6:38

GOD DESIRES OUR OBEDIENCE

He who loves father or mother more than Me is not worthy of Me; and he who loves son or daughter more than Me is not worthy of Me. And he who does not take his cross and follow after Me is not worthy of Me. He who has found his life shall lose it, and he who has lost his life for My sake shall find it.   *Matt. 10:37–39*

For whoever does the will of My Father who is in heaven, he is My brother and sister and mother.   *Matt. 12:50*

For whoever does the will of God, he is My brother and sister and mother.   *Mark 3:35*

But He said, "On the contrary, blessed are those who hear the word of God, and observe it."
                                                    Luke 11:28

And He summoned the multitude with His disciples, and said to them, "If anyone wishes to come after Me, let him deny himself, and take up his cross, and follow Me. For whoever wishes to save his life shall lose it; and whoever loses his life for My sake and the gospel's shall save it. For what does it profit a man to gain the whole world, and forfeit his soul? For what shall a man give in exchange for his soul? For whoever is ashamed of Me and My words in this adulterous and sinful generation, the Son of Man will also be ashamed of him when He comes in the glory of His Father with the holy angels."
                                                    Mark 8:34–38

And He was saying to them all, "If anyone wishes to come after Me, let him deny himself, and take up his cross daily, and follow Me. For whoever wishes to save his life shall lose it, but whoever loses his life for My sake, he is the one who will save it. For what is a man profited if he gains the whole world, and loses or forfeits himself? For whoever is ashamed of Me and My words, of him will the Son of Man be ashamed when He comes in His glory, and the glory of the Father and of the holy angels."   *Luke 9:23–26*

He who loves his life loses it; and he who hates his life in this world shall keep it to life eternal. If anyone serves Me, let him follow Me; and where I am, there shall My servant also be; if anyone serves Me, the Father will honor him.
                                                    John 12:25–26

CHAPTER SEVEN

SELF-EXAMINATION:
HONESTLY EXPLORING OUR SIN

CHRISTIAN PRINCIPLE: SELF-EXAMINATION	AA'S STEP FOUR	CHRISTIAN ADAPTATION
Let us examine and probe our ways, and let us return to the Lord. *Lam. 3:40* But let a man examine himself. *1 Cor. 11:28*	Made a searching and fearless moral inventory of ourselves.	Honestly examined the impact of sin in our lives.

A Saturday morning family ritual is to clean house before doing something fun. As one Saturday morning drew to a close, I asked my daughter, Christine, if her room was clean. "Do you want to know the truth?" was her odd but revealing answer. In one brief statement she suggested that I could choose to walk down one of two paths—deception or truth. If I desired, she would tell me what I wanted to hear, which in this case was a far cry from her room's actual condition. The second path, the path of truth, would allow us respond to and amend the existing circumstances.

The process of sanctification requires a willingness to know the truth about our sin. God requires our willing cooperation in its removal; but removal of sin is impossible without an understanding of sin.

This knowledge is available only through a fearless and searching self-examination! We must boldly hold up a spiritual mirror to our soul and take a good, hard look. Our goal is to see who God wants us to become, determine where we fall short, and use that information as the basis for future change. We must inspect, in great detail, words, intentions, and behavior to determine where, how, and why they contradict God's will for our lives.

Self-examination is the natural outcome of a repentant heart. Our desire to live for Christ must always be followed with action based on knowledge. A thorough self-examination is designed to provide the required knowledge. We ask ourselves: "What changes does God require of me? What behaviors and attitudes does He want me to eliminate? How does my life differ today from the life He is calling me to live tomorrow?"

Looking truthfully at our sin can be painful. Frequently we prefer the other path, the path of self-deception. Like alcoholics who drink daily, drive drunk, verbally abuse their family, and yet deny their drinking problem, we Christians often deny the sin in our lives. We paint a false mental picture of our lives and ignore anything that contradicts our self-imposed illusion. We are proud but believe we are humble, we are selfish but believe we are loving, we are angry but believe we are honest. This self-deception hinders our Christian life. The intimacy that God desires with us is no more than a nice idea as long as we deny our sin.

Human potential for self-deception can at times be humorous. Since my youth I have feared becoming bald. Those fears seemed justified—my father and both my grandfathers had little or no hair on the top of their heads. As I aged, I hoped against hope that I would not become the next victim of this "Selby curse." I held my own until about the age of thirty. Then, gradually, more and more hair began to make way for my scalp. Fortunately, most of my initial hair loss was restricted to the back of my head. To this day a tuft of hair still resides two inches above my eyes. These stubborn hairs assisted my denial. Whenever looking in a mirror, if I angled my face upward, I could effectively hide the growing circle of shiny skin on the back of my head.

This self-deception worked perfectly well until one unfortunate day. As I sat on the floor playing with my kids, they said in unison at the top of their lungs, "Dad, your bald spot is getting bigger." My self-deception was instantly vaporized and replaced with a painful dose of reality.

What was I to do? How should I deal with the unpleasant circumstances and facts thrown at me? Should I stop playing with my kids, or perhaps never sit on the floor again? Or maybe I could threaten to punish my children if they ever dared to say such a terrible thing again. Or perhaps I could try to accept the reality of my situation.

Self-examination will not eliminate bald spots but will help eliminate blind spots. God is willing to replace our denial with reality. Fueled by our courage to know the truth, God will graciously point out behaviors and attitudes that are inconsistent with His will for us and enable us to change.

Some say ignorance is bliss, but not so when dealing with sin. It is always a destructive force that has painful consequences. It damages our relationships with others. It diminishes the quality of our life and distances us from God. If we participate in sinful behavior yet believe it not sinful, we still reap the consequences of that behavior.

In ages past physicians believed that bloodletting was a helpful form of medical treatment. They sincerely believed they helped their patients by cutting holes in their body and allowing large quantities of blood to flow out. In this case ignorance, even innocent, well-meaning ignorance, produced the opposite result from that intended. Instead of providing life, it led to destruction. Similarly, Christians are reaping the consequences of sinful behaviors that they have yet to realize are sinful.

Knowledge of God's word, the Bible, is an indispensable element of self-examination. His words enlighten, convict, and direct us. His commands make clear His intentions for us. Without knowing His word, how can we know His will? Without knowing His will, how can we know our sin? We must know His word to know our sin.

Sin takes a number of different forms. Some sins are obvious; they are behaviors that are clearly contrary to God's will and His Word. God tells us, "You shall not steal."[1] So if we steal, we sin—obviously. God tells us we shall not bear false testimony, so if we lie, we sin. The more familiar we become with God's will and word, the easier it becomes for us to identify behavioral sins.

Other sin is far subtler. It exists exclusively in our hearts, visible to no one but God and us. God is concerned about our hearts—that is, our thoughts, intentions, and desires. Jesus was constantly critical of first-century religious leaders because many pretended to honor God externally, but deep within their hearts they were filled with greed. This hypocrisy is not suitable for God's people. God desires integrity between our hearts and our actions. In fact, He declares that our hearts will determine our actions.[2]

Self-examination requires that we explore the inner recesses of our being. What are our intentions, desires, values, and how do these coincide with God's will for us? We may not sexually sin with our body, but what about in our mind? We may not audibly curse our enemies, but do we despise them in our heart? These are examples of the type of internal exploration that self-examination demands.

Sin is not always active. Many times we sin by doing nothing—that is, by not doing what God directs us to do. These types of sins are often called sins of omission and are perfectly described by James, who proclaims:

> Therefore, to one who knows the right thing to do, and does not do it, to him it is sin.[3]

If God directs me to love my wife, and I ignore her—I sin. If God directs me to give to those in need, and I ignore those in need—I sin. So sins of omission must also be considered as we examine ourselves.

Prayer is indispensable in the process of self-examination. Seek God's assistance to examine your mind and heart. Ask Him to provide the willingness to be honest about your sin, so you might change. Consider the prayers of the psalmist as a model for yourself:

> Examine me, O Lord, and try me; test my mind and my heart.[4]

Self-examination is often painful, but it need not be fearful. As you proceed, remember that God loves you. He knows your sins—all of them—and He still loves you. His love is not conditional. He does not grade on a curve, and His purpose is always redemptive to those who are His. Those who have received the mercy and forgiveness of Christ need not be concerned with God's rejection. Armed with this truth, we can courageously begin the process of self-examination.

Insights from our self-examination should be

---

1. Matthew 19:18
2. See verses at the end of the chapter.
3. James 4:17
4. Ps. 26:2

written. This is helpful for a number of reasons. A written inventory provides the opportunity to concretely recognize areas in your life where God desires to see change. A written record will enable you more effectively to apply the remaining other spiritual disciplines described in later chapters. A number of exercises are provided at the end of this chapter to help you write down areas of your life that are contrary to God's will.

Prayerfully consider how long you will devote yourself to this process of self-examination. But beware of procrastination. Give yourself a time frame for completion. I suggest at least two weeks, but no more then a month. The worksheets included at the end of this chapter will provide you with a helpful structure.

Reviewing key Bible passages will be particularly helpful as you begin your process of self-examination. Read slowly, prayerfully, and thoughtfully the following sections of the Bible as you proceed.

1. The Sermon on the Mount, Matthew 5, 6, and 7, which addresses the inner as well as the external workings of sin
2. The entire book of James, which focuses on practical Christian living
3. 1 Corinthians 13, often called "The Love Chapter"; it provides the reader with a positive example of behavior to compare ourselves with
4. 1 John, which clearly outlines certain sinful behaviors

Self-examination is not an end in itself. It will be followed by other disciplines designed by God to assist in your sanctification.

SELF-EXAMINATION WORKSHEET
FOR GROUP DISCUSSION AND PERSONAL REFLECTION

1. **Read Luke 18:9–14, and discuss the following questions.**

Describe the different attitudes between the Pharisee and the tax collector.

What factors contributed to the Pharisee's denial of his sin?

What factors contributed to God's acceptance of the tax collector's prayers?

2. **John tells us that if we say we have no sin, we deceive ourselves. In your opinion why do Christians at times deny their sin?**

3. **Based on the following scriptures, describe what factors contribute to and reflect self-deception?**

For if anyone thinks he is something when he is nothing, he deceives himself.

Gal. 6:3

But prove yourselves doers of the word, and not merely hearers who delude themselves.

James 1:22

If anyone thinks himself to be religious, and yet does not bridle his tongue but deceives his own heart, this man's religion is worthless.

James 1:26

4. **Read the scripture below and answer the following questions.**

And this is the judgment, that the light is come into the world, and men loved the darkness rather than the light; for their deeds were evil. For everyone who does evil hates the light, and does not come to the light, lest his deeds should be exposed. But he who practices the truth comes to the light, that his deeds may be manifested as having been wrought in God.

John 3:19–21

What does "come to the light" mean?

Who chooses to come into the light? Who chooses not to come into the light?

SELF-EXAMINATION WORKSHEETS
FOR PERSONAL REFLECTION ONLY

A clear vision of our desired outcome immeasurably aids effective self-examination. The more clearly we understand who God desires that we become, the more clearly we see our shortcomings. Our model for Christian living is Christ Himself. He is our standard.

In many different ways, in many different words, we are repeatedly told the same thing—Christians are to become like Christ.[5] As God's children, we are directed to become like Him.

God is light, and in Him is no darkness. He is sinless, holy, merciful, and righteous. Just as He is pure, His desire is that we purify ourselves. Just as He is in the light, we must walk in the light. Just as He is holy, we must be holy. Just as He is righteous, we, too, must become righteous. Our process of self-examination must be done with the standard of His holiness in mind.

This may seem impossible. How can we mere humans become like Christ? The answer is we can't—not by our own strength. Our determination alone is grossly inadequate to make the changes that God requires. But we are not alone in this effort. We have a powerful partner who dwells within us—God Himself. Our purification, our ability to become like Him, come from His power that dwells within us.[6] Believers who have sincerely committed their lives to Christ can be assured of God's indwelling presence. God's indwelling Spirit enables us to see our sin honestly and provides us the desire and ability to be transformed into the image of Christ.

The following exercise will help you consider some of the character traits of Christ that should be evident in His followers. Each page asks you to consider your present exercise of a particular Christlike characteristic. This is by no means a complete list of character traits, yet by completing this exercise you will see more clearly who God wants you to become and where you fall short.

---

5. See verses at the end of the chapter.
6. Ibid.

CHRISTLIKE TRAITS OF COMPASSION AND MERCY	
COMPASSION AND MERCY	RELATED SCRIPTURE
Feeling of sympathy for others and awareness of their pain	But go and learn what this means, "I desire compassion, and not sacrifice," for I did not come to call the righteous, but sinners. *Matt. 9:13* Be merciful, just as your Father is merciful. *Luke 6:36*
CIRCLE FREQUENCY PRACTICED.	NEVER RARELY SOMETIMES OFTEN ALWAYS
List examples of compassion and mercy in your life. (Use more paper if needed.)	
List times that you lacked this trait when you should have exercised it.	

CHRISTLIKE TRAIT OF KINDNESS	
KINDNESS	RELATED SCRIPTURE
The steadfast love that maintains relationships through gracious aid in times of need	But the fruit of the Spirit is love, joy, peace, patience, kindness, goodness, faithfulness. *Gal. 5:22* And so, as those who have been chosen of God, holy and beloved, put on a heart of compassion, kindness, humility, gentleness and patience. *Col. 3:12*
CIRCLE FREQUENCY PRACTICED.	NEVER RARELY SOMETIMES OFTEN ALWAYS
List examples of kindness in your life. (Use more paper if needed.)	
List times that you lacked this trait when you should have exercised it.	

CHRISTLIKE TRAIT OF HUMILITY	
HUMILITY	RELATED SCRIPTURE
The recognition of one's limitations, dependence on God, and respect for others	My people who are called by My name humble themselves and pray, and seek My face and turn from their wicked ways, then I will hear from heaven, will forgive their sin, and will heal their land. *2 Chron. 7:14* For everyone who exalts himself shall be humbled, and he who humbles himself shall be exalted. *Luke 14:11*
CIRCLE FREQUENCY PRACTICED.	NEVER RARELY SOMETIMES OFTEN ALWAYS
List examples of humility in your life. (Use more paper if needed.)	
List times that you lacked this trait when you should have exercised it.	

CHRISTLIKE TRAITS OF PATIENCE AND LONG-SUFFERING

PATIENCE AND LONG-SUFFERING	RELATED SCRIPTURE
Slowness to anger and willingness to deal with people and situations in a kind and thoughtful way over an extended period of time	. . . in purity, in knowledge, in patience, in kindness, in the Holy Spirit, in genuine love . . . *2 Cor. 6:6* But the fruit of the Spirit is love, joy, peace, patience, kindness, goodness, faithfulness. *Gal. 5:22* Consider it all joy, my brethren, when you encounter various trials, knowing that the testing of your faith produces endurance. And let endurance have its perfect result, that you may be perfect and complete, lacking in nothing. *James 1:2–4*
CIRCLE FREQUENCY PRACTICED.	NEVER RARELY SOMETIMES OFTEN ALWAYS
List examples of patience in your life. (Use more paper if needed.)	
List times that you lacked this trait when you should have exercised it.	

CHRISTLIKE TRAIT OF SELF-CONTROL

SELF-CONTROL	RELATED SCRIPTURE
The ability to resist destructive impulses	Like a city that is broken into and without walls Is a man who has no control over his spirit. *Prov. 25:28* . . . gentleness, self-control; against such things there is no law. *Gal. 5:23* . . . loving what is good, sensible, just, devout, self-controlled . . . *Titus 1:8*
CIRCLE FREQUENCY PRACTICED.	NEVER RARELY SOMETIMES OFTEN ALWAYS
List examples of self-control in your life. (Use more paper if needed.)	
List times that you lacked this trait when you should have exercised it.	

CHRISTLIKE TRAIT OF FORGIVENESS	
FORGIVENESS	RELATED SCRIPTURE
Not holding someone accountable for wrongdoing	For if you forgive men for their transgressions, your heavenly Father will also forgive you. But if you do not forgive men, then your Father will not forgive your transgressions. *Matt. 6:14–15* And whenever you stand praying, forgive, if you have anything against anyone; so that your Father also who is in heaven may forgive you your transgressions. But if you do not forgive, neither will your Father who is in heaven forgive your transgressions. *Mark 11:25–26* And be kind to one another, tender-hearted, forgiving each other, just as God in Christ also has forgiven you. *Eph. 4:32*
CIRCLE FREQUENCY PRACTICED.	NEVER RARELY SOMETIMES OFTEN ALWAYS
List examples of forgiveness in your life. (Use more paper if needed.)	
List times that you lacked this trait when you should have exercised it.	

CHRISTLIKE TRAIT OF FAITH	
FAITH	RELATED SCRIPTURE
A trusting commitment to God in all circumstances, both positive and negative	Now faith is the assurance of things hoped for, the conviction of things not seen. *Heb. 11:1*
CIRCLE FREQUENCY PRACTICED.	NEVER RARELY SOMETIMES OFTEN ALWAYS
List examples of faith in your life. (Use more paper if needed.)	
List times that you lacked this trait when you should have exercised it.	

SELF-EXAMINATION WORKSHEETS
FOR PERSONAL REFLECTION AND APPLICATION

The next self-examination worksheets challenge us to look at sin. You will familiarize yourself with biblical sin and will consider your level of participation. Prayerfully consider the sin's name and definition, then indicate your degree of participation. This is not a complete list of sin, but it summarizes a number of sins prevalent in biblical times as well as our day. Use the following grids as only a starting point. You can expand the grids on your own paper to be more comprehensive.

Sin is almost always reflected by what we think, say, and what we do, so I have categorized sin in three ways: sins of the heart, behavioral sins, and sins of the mouth.

The first grid examines sins of the heart. These are the sins that no one sees but God and you.

SINS OF THE HEART

> For from within, out of the heart of men, proceed the evil thoughts and fornications, thefts, murders, adulteries, deeds of coveting and wickedness, as well as deceit, sensuality, envy, slander, pride and foolishness.[7]

Sin is most evident through actions and words. Yet all sin has its root in the heart. A thorough self-examination of sin must begin with an honest analysis of thoughts and attitudes that are contrary to God's will and purpose for His people. The next set of worksheets defines sins of the heart and provides you the opportunity to evaluate your participation in them. This is not meant to be an exhaustive or complete list of sins of the heart. Yet it will give you helpful information regarding attitudes that God would have you repent of. Some of these sins are likely more prevalent in your life than others are. Just try to be as complete as you can.

---

7. Mark 7:21–22

IDOLATRY	
IDOLATRY	RELATED SCRIPTURE
Any preoccupation that takes precedence over our commitment to God; money, possessions, television, hobbies, even other people can be an idol	No one can serve two masters; for either he will hate the one and love the other, or he will hold to one and despise the other. You cannot serve God and mammon. *Matt. 6:24* For this you know with certainty, that no immoral or impure person or covetous man, who is an idolater, has an inheritance in the kingdom of Christ and God. *Eph. 5:5*
CIRCLE FREQUENCY PRACTICED.	NEVER RARELY SOMETIMES OFTEN ALWAYS
List examples of idolatry in your life. (Use more paper if needed.)	
Describe how this sin has affected your relationship with God. (Use more paper if needed.)	

| Describe how this sin has affected your relationships with other people.
(Use more paper if needed.) | |

PRIDE	
PRIDE	RELATED SCRIPTURE
The elevation of self, the belief in your own abilities as opposed to a dependence on God; is exhibited by disrespect to authority, seeking the approval of humans, reluctance to serve, and making unreasonable demands on others	For everyone who exalts himself shall be humbled, but he who humbles himself shall be exalted. *Luke 18:14* You younger men, likewise, be subject to your elders; and all of you, clothe yourselves with humility toward one another, for God is opposed to the proud, but gives grace to the humble. *1 Pet. 5:5*
CIRCLE FREQUENCY PRACTICED.	NEVER RARELY SOMETIMES OFTEN ALWAYS
List examples of pride in your life. (Use more paper if needed.)	
Describe how this sin has affected your relationship with God. (Use more paper if needed.)	

| Describe how this sin has affected your relationships with other people. (Use more paper if needed.) | |

UNFORGIVENESS

UNFORGIVENESS	RELATED SCRIPTURE
Unwillingness to forgive, which causes bitterness, ill feelings, and distances us from God	For if you forgive men for their transgressions, your heavenly Father will also forgive you. But if you do not forgive men, then your Father will not forgive your transgressions. *Matt. 6:14–15* And be kind to one another, tender-hearted, forgiving each other, just as God in Christ also has forgiven you. *Eph. 4:32*
CIRCLE FREQUENCY PRACTICED.	NEVER RARELY SOMETIMES OFTEN ALWAYS
List examples of unforgiveness in your life. (Use more paper if needed.)	
Describe how this sin has affected your relationship with God. (Use more paper if needed.)	

Describe how this sin has affected your relationships with other people. (Use more paper if needed.)	

GREED AND COVETING	
GREED AND COVETING	RELATED SCRIPTURE
Excessive interest in acquiring things or money	And He said to them, "Beware, and be on your guard against every form of greed; for not even when one has an abundance does his life consist of his possessions." *Luke 12:15* Let your way of life be free from the love of money, being content with what you have; for He Himself has said, "I will never desert you, nor will I ever forsake you." *Heb. 13:5*
CIRCLE FREQUENCY PRACTICED.	NEVER RARELY SOMETIMES OFTEN ALWAYS
List examples of greed and coveting in your life. (Use more paper if needed.)	
Describe how this sin has affected your relationship with God. (Use more paper if needed.)	

Describe how this sin has affected your relationships with other people. (Use more paper if needed.)	

ANXIETY AND FEAR	
ANXIETY AND FEAR	RELATED SCRIPTURE
Fears about present or future, reflecting both a dependence on self and distrust in God	Do not be anxious then, saying, "What shall we eat?" or "What shall we drink?" or "With what shall we clothe ourselves?" For all these things the Gentiles eagerly seek; for your heavenly Father knows that you need all these things. But seek first His kingdom and His righteousness; and all these things shall be added to you. Therefore do not be anxious for tomorrow; for tomorrow will care for itself. Each day has enough trouble of its own. *Matt. 6:31–34* Be anxious for nothing, but in everything by prayer and supplication with thanksgiving let your requests be made known to God. *Phil. 4:6*
CIRCLE FREQUENCY PRACTICED.	NEVER RARELY SOMETIMES OFTEN ALWAYS
List examples of anxiety and fear in your life. (Use more paper if needed.)	
Describe how this sin has affected your relationship with God. (Use more paper if needed.)	

Describe how this sin has affected your relationships with other people. (Use more paper if needed.)	

SEXUAL LUST	
SEXUAL LUST	RELATED SCRIPTURE
Not being focused on things that are pure; having sinful sexual fantasies	But I say to you, that everyone who looks on a woman to lust for her has committed adultery with her already in his heart. *Matt. 5:28* Finally, brethren, whatever is true, whatever is honorable, whatever is right, whatever is pure, whatever is lovely, whatever is of good repute, if there is any excellence and if anything worthy of praise, let your mind dwell on these things. *Phil. 4:8*
CIRCLE FREQUENCY PRACTICED.	NEVER RARELY SOMETIMES OFTEN ALWAYS
List examples of sexual lust in your life. (Use more paper if needed.)	
Describe how this sin has affected your relationship with God. (Use more paper if needed.)	

Describe how this sin has affected your relationships with other people. (Use more paper if needed.)	

SELFISHNESS

SELFISHNESS	RELATED SCRIPTURE
Not being sensitive and responsive to the needs of others; preoccupation with self	Do nothing from selfishness or empty conceit, but with humility of mind let each of you regard one another as more important than himself. *Phil. 2:3* For they all seek after their own interests, not those of Christ Jesus. *Phil. 2:21*
CIRCLE FREQUENCY PRACTICED.	NEVER RARELY SOMETIMES OFTEN ALWAYS
List examples of selfishness in your life. (Use more paper if needed.)	
Describe how this sin has affected your relationship with God. (Use more paper if needed.)	

Describe how this sin has affected your relationships with other people. (Use more paper if needed.)	

ENVY	
ENVY	RELATED SCRIPTURE
Sinful desire for what others have; we can envy someone's job, lifestyle, family, possessions, etc. Envy causes conflict and reflects contempt for God's provision in our life	Let us not become boastful, challenging one another, envying one another. *Gal. 5:26* For we also once were foolish ourselves, disobedient, deceived, enslaved to various lusts and pleasures, spending our life in malice and envy, hateful, hating one another. *Titus 3:3*
CIRCLE FREQUENCY PRACTICED.	NEVER RARELY SOMETIMES OFTEN ALWAYS
List examples of envy in your life. (Use more paper if needed.)	
Describe how this sin has affected your relationship with God. (Use more paper if needed.)	

Describe how this sin has affected your relationships with other people. (Use more paper if needed.)	

GUILE AND DECEIT

GUILE AND DECEIT	RELATED SCRIPTURE
The willful desire to deceive others for one's own benefit	You are of your father the devil, and you want to do the desires of your father. He was a murderer from the beginning, and does not stand in the truth, because there is no truth in him. Whenever he speaks a lie, he speaks from his own nature; for he is a liar, and the father of lies. *John 8:44* Therefore, putting aside all malice and all guile and hypocrisy and envy and all slander . . . *1 Pet. 2:1*
CIRCLE FREQUENCY PRACTICED.	NEVER RARELY SOMETIMES OFTEN ALWAYS
List examples of guile and deceit in your life. (Use more paper if needed.)	
Describe how this sin has affected your relationship with God. (Use more paper if needed.)	

Describe how this sin has affected your relationships with other people. (Use more paper if needed.)	

MALICE	
MALICE	RELATED SCRIPTURE
The harboring of ill will toward others with the intention to harm them	For we also once were foolish ourselves, disobedient, deceived, enslaved to various lusts and pleasures, spending our life in malice and envy, hateful, hating one another. *Titus 3:3* Therefore, putting aside all malice and all guile and hypocrisy and envy and all slander . . . *1 Pet. 2:1*
CIRCLE FREQUENCY PRACTICED.	NEVER RARELY SOMETIMES OFTEN ALWAYS
List examples of malice in your life. (Use more paper if needed.)	
Describe how this sin has affected your relationship with God. (Use more paper if needed.)	

Describe how this sin has affected your relationships with other people. (Use more paper if needed.)	

PREJUDICE AND PARTIALITY	
PREJUDICE AND PARTIALITY	RELATED SCRIPTURE
Preferred treatment based on wealth, gender, race, social class, etc.	For if a man comes into your assembly with a gold ring and dressed in fine clothes, and there also comes in a poor man in dirty clothes, and you pay special attention to the one who is wearing the fine clothes, and say, "You sit here in a good place," and you say to the poor man, "You stand over there, or sit down by my footstool," have you not made distinctions among yourselves, and become judges with evil motives? *James 2:2–4* But if you show partiality, you are committing sin and are convicted by the law as transgressors. *James 2:9*
CIRCLE FREQUENCY PRACTICED.	NEVER RARELY SOMETIMES OFTEN ALWAYS
List examples of prejudice and partiality in your life. (Use more paper if needed.)	
Describe how this sin has affected your relationship with God. (Use more paper if needed.)	

Describe how this sin has affected your relationships with other people. (Use more paper if needed.)	

BEHAVIORAL SINS

Sin has its roots in our heart but rarely exists there alone. Sinful thoughts and desires will almost always be reflected in what we say and do. A thorough self-examination must always include an honest evaluation of our behavior.

Behavioral sins are broken into two types: what we say and what we do. Complete these worksheets as thoroughly as possible.

STEALING	
STEALING	RELATED SCRIPTURE
Taking anything that does not belong to you; this includes material possessions as well as time owed to an employer; covetousness, greed, and selfishness typically aid stealing	You know the commandments, "Do not murder, Do not commit adultery, Do not steal, Do not bear false witness, Do not defraud, Honor your father and mother." *Mark 10:19* Let him who steals steal no longer; but rather let him labor, performing with his own hands what is good, in order that he may have something to share with him who has need. *Eph. 4:28*
CIRCLE FREQUENCY PRACTICED.	NEVER RARELY SOMETIMES OFTEN ALWAYS
List examples of stealing in your life. (Use more paper if needed.)	
Describe how this sin has affected your relationship with God. (Use more paper if needed.)	

Describe how this sin has affected your relationships with other people. (Use more paper if needed.)	

ANGER AND VIOLENCE

ANGER AND VIOLENCE	RELATED SCRIPTURE
Lack of self-control in all situations; anger and violence typically reflect selfishness or resentments	But I say to you that every one who is angry with his brother shall be guilty before the court; and whoever shall say to his brother, "Raca," shall be guilty before the supreme court; and whoever shall say, "You fool," shall be guilty enough to go into the hell of fire. *Matt. 5:22* Be angry, and yet do not sin; do not let the sun go down on your anger. *Eph. 4:26* But now you also, put them all aside: anger, wrath, malice, slander, and abusive speech from your mouth. *Col. 3:8*
CIRCLE FREQUENCY PRACTICED.	NEVER RARELY SOMETIMES OFTEN ALWAYS
List examples of anger and violence in your life. (Use more paper if needed.)	
Describe how this sin has affected your relationship with God. (Use more paper if needed.)	

Describe how this sin has affected your relationships with other people. (Use more paper if needed.)	

SEXUAL SIN	
SEXUAL SIN	RELATED SCRIPTURE
Sexual behavior outside of marriage, including premarital and extramarital sexuality as well as pornography; it reflects of covetousness and lust	Flee immorality. Every other sin that a man commits is outside the body, but the immoral man sins against his own body. Or do you not know that your body is a temple of the Holy Spirit who is in you, whom you have from God, and that you are not your own? *1 Cor. 6:18–19* Let marriage be held in honor among all, and let the marriage bed be undefiled; for fornicators and adulterers God will judge. *Heb. 13:4*
CIRCLE FREQUENCY PRACTICED.	NEVER RARELY SOMETIMES OFTEN ALWAYS
List examples of sexual sin in your life. (Use more paper if needed.)	
Describe how this sin has affected your relationship with God. (Use more paper if needed.)	

Describe how this sin has affected your relationships with other people. (Use more paper if needed.)	

HOARDING

HOARDING	RELATED SCRIPTURE
Putting our trust in possessions instead of God	Do not lay up for yourselves treasures upon earth, where moth and rust destroy, and where thieves break in and steal. But lay up for yourselves treasures in heaven, where neither moth nor rust destroys, and where thieves do not break in or steal; for where your treasure is, there will your heart be also. *Matt. 6:19–21* Instruct those who are rich in this present world not to be conceited or to fix their hope on the uncertainty of riches, but on God, who richly supplies us with all things to enjoy. *1 Tim. 6:17*
CIRCLE FREQUENCY PRACTICED.	NEVER RARELY SOMETIMES OFTEN ALWAYS
List examples of hoarding in your life. (Use more paper if needed.)	
Describe how this sin has affected your relationship with God. (Use more paper if needed.)	

Describe how this sin has affected your relationships with other people. (Use more paper if needed.)	

OCCULT PRACTICES

OCCULT PRACTICES	RELATED SCRIPTURE
Contact with spiritual forces other than God Himself including magic, witchcraft, sorcery, divination as well as other occult practices	Do not turn to mediums or spiritists; do not seek them out to be defiled by them. I am the Lord your God. *Lev. 19:31* And many of those who practiced magic brought their books together and began burning them in the sight of all; and they counted up the price of them and found it fifty thousand pieces of silver. *Acts 19:19*
CIRCLE FREQUENCY PRACTICED.	NEVER RARELY SOMETIMES OFTEN ALWAYS
List examples of occult practices in your life. (Use more paper if needed.)	
Describe how this sin has affected your relationship with God. (Use more paper if needed.)	

Describe how this sin has affected your relationships with other people. (Use more paper if needed.)	

SINS OF THE TONGUE

Our words will always give us away. They reflect the condition of our heart. As part of our self-examination we must closely examine what we say and determine if our words are contrary to God's will. Numerous scriptures highlight the importance of our words.

> You brood of vipers, how can you, being evil, speak what is good? For the mouth speaks out of that which fills the heart.[8]

> And I say to you, that every careless word that men shall speak, they shall render account for it in the day of judgment.[9]

> The good man out of the good treasure of his heart brings forth what is good; and the evil man out of the evil treasure brings forth what is evil; for his mouth speaks from that which fills his heart.[10]

> So also the tongue is a small part of the body, and yet it boasts of great things. Behold, how great a forest is set aflame by such a small fire! And the tongue is a fire, the very world of iniquity; the tongue is set among our members as that which defiles the entire body, and sets on fire the course of our life, and is set on fire by hell.[11]

---

8. Matt. 12:36
9. Matt. 12:34
10. Luke 6:45
11. James 3:5–6

SLANDER

SLANDER	RELATED SCRIPTURE
Speaking critically of another person, which intentionally or unintentionally results in destroying their character; often reflects malice, envy, or bitterness	Women must likewise be dignified, not malicious gossips, but temperate, faithful in all things. *1 Tim. 3:11* Do not speak against one another, brethren. He who speaks against a brother, or judges his brother, speaks against the law, and judges the law; but if you judge the law, you are not a doer of the law, but a judge of it. *James 4:11* Therefore, putting aside all malice and all guile and hypocrisy and envy and all slander . . . *1 Pet. 2:1*
CIRCLE FREQUENCY PRACTICED.	NEVER RARELY SOMETIMES OFTEN ALWAYS
List examples of slander in your life. (Use more paper if needed.)	
Describe how this sin has affected your relationship with God. (Use more paper if needed.)	

Describe how this sin has affected your relationships with other people. (Use more paper if needed.)	

LYING AND DECEPTION

LYING AND DECEPTION	RELATED SCRIPTURE
Deceptive, dishonest, or false words that reflect guile, anxiety or fear, malice, or pride	Therefore, laying aside falsehood, speak truth, each one of you, with his neighbor, for we are members of one another. *Eph. 4:25* Do not lie to one another, since you laid aside the old self with its evil practices. *Col. 3:9*
CIRCLE FREQUENCY PRACTICED.	NEVER RARELY SOMETIMES OFTEN ALWAYS
List examples of lying and deception in your life. (Use more paper if needed.)	
Describe how this sin has affected your relationship with God. (Use more paper if needed.)	

Describe how this sin has affected your relationships with other people. (Use more paper if needed.)	

COMPLAINING

COMPLAINING	RELATED SCRIPTURE
Not being thankful to God in all things, reflecting a lack of faith	Nor grumble, as some of them did, and were destroyed by the destroyer. *1 Cor. 10:10* Do all things without grumbling or disputing. *Phil. 2:14* Do not complain, brethren, against one another, that you yourselves may not be judged; behold, the Judge is standing right at the door. *James 5:9* In everything give thanks; for this is God's will for you in Christ Jesus. *1 Thess. 5:18*
CIRCLE FREQUENCY PRACTICED.	NEVER RARELY SOMETIMES OFTEN ALWAYS
List examples of complaining in your life. (Use more paper if needed.)	
Describe how this sin has affected your relationship with God. (Use more paper if needed.)	

Describe how this sin has affected your relationships with other people. (Use more paper if needed.)	

USING GOD'S NAME IN VAIN

USING GOD'S NAME IN VAIN	RELATED SCRIPTURE
Referring to God in a common or casual way without respect and reverence	You shall not take the name of the Lord your God in vain, for the Lord will not leave him unpunished who takes His name in vain. *Exod. 20: 7* But above all, my brethren, do not swear, either by heaven or by earth or with any other oath; but let your yes be yes, and your no, no; so that you may not fall under judgment. *James 5:12*
CIRCLE FREQUENCY PRACTICED.	NEVER RARELY SOMETIMES OFTEN ALWAYS
List examples of using God's name in vain in your life. (Use more paper if needed.)	
Describe how this sin has affected your relationship with God. (Use more paper if needed.)	

Describe how this sin has affected your relationships with other people. (Use more paper if needed.)	

FLATTERY	
FLATTERY	RELATED SCRIPTURE
Seeking approval for unwholesome purposes; using manipulation to deceive others	For such men are slaves not of our Lord Christ but of their own appetites; and by their smooth and flattering speech they deceive the hearts of the unsuspecting. *Rom. 16:18* These are grumblers, finding fault, following after their own lusts; they speak arrogantly, flattering people for the sake of gaining an advantage. *Jude 1:16*
CIRCLE FREQUENCY PRACTICED.	NEVER RARELY SOMETIMES OFTEN ALWAYS
List examples of flattery in your life. (Use more paper if needed.)	
Describe how this sin has affected your relationship with God. (Use more paper if needed.)	

Describe how this sin has affected your relationships with other people. (Use more paper if needed.)	

COARSE JOKING AND VULGARITY

COARSE JOKING AND VULGARITY	RELATED SCRIPTURE
Hurtful comments and jokes that belittle people	Let no unwholesome word proceed from your mouth, but only such a word as is good for edification according to the need of the moment, that it may give grace to those who hear. *Eph. 4:29* And there must be no filthiness and silly talk, or coarse jesting, which are not fitting, but rather giving of thanks. *Eph. 5:4*
CIRCLE FREQUENCY PRACTICED.	NEVER RARELY SOMETIMES OFTEN ALWAYS
List examples of coarse joking and vulgarity in your life. (Use more paper if needed.)	
Describe how this sin has affected your relationship with God. (Use more paper if needed.)	

Describe how this sin has affected your relationships with other people. (Use more paper if needed.)	

SCRIPTURES RELATED TO SELF-EXAMINATION

GENERAL SCRIPTURES ON SELF-EXAMINATION

How many are my iniquities and sins? Make known to me my rebellion and my sin.

Job 13:23

Examine me, O Lord, and try me; Test my mind and my heart.

Ps. 26:2

Search me, O God, and know my heart; Try me and know my anxious thoughts; and see if there be any hurtful way in me, and lead me in the everlasting way.

Ps. 139:23–24

The heart is more deceitful than all else and is desperately sick; Who can understand it?

Jer. 17:9

Let us examine and probe our ways, and let us return to the Lord.

Lam. 3:40

Thus says the Lord of hosts, "Consider your ways!"

Hag. 1:7

But let a man examine himself, and so let him eat of the bread and drink of the cup.

1 Cor. 11:28

But if we judged ourselves rightly, we should not be judged.

1 Cor. 11:31

Test yourselves to see if you are in the faith; examine yourselves! Or do you not recognize this about yourselves, that Jesus Christ is in you—unless indeed you fail the test? *2 Cor. 13:5*

For if anyone thinks he is something when he is nothing, he deceives himself. But let each one examine his own work, and then he will have reason for boasting in regard to himself alone, and not in regard to another. For each one shall bear his own load.

Gal. 6:3–5

MOTIVES OF THE HEART

This people honors Me with their lips, but their heart is far away from me. *Matt. 15:8*

But the things that proceed out of the mouth come from the heart, and those defile the man.

Matt. 15:18

Woe to you, scribes and Pharisees, hypocrites! For you are like whitewashed tombs which on the outside appear beautiful, but inside they are full of dead men's bones and all uncleanness. Even so you too outwardly appear righteous to men, but inwardly you are full of hypocrisy and lawlessness. *Matt. 23:27–28*

The good man out of the good treasure of his heart brings forth what is good; and the evil man out of the evil treasure brings forth what is evil; for his mouth speaks from that which fills his heart. *Luke 6:45*

THE CHRISTIAN CHARACTER

But the fruit of the Spirit is love, joy, peace, patience, kindness, goodness, faithfulness, gentleness, self-control; against such things there is no law. Now those who belong to Christ Jesus have crucified the flesh with its passions and desires. *Gal. 5:22–24*

And so, as those who have been chosen of God, holy and beloved, put on a heart of compassion, kindness, humility, gentleness and patience; bearing with one another, and forgiving each other, whoever has a complaint against anyone; just as the Lord forgave you, so also should you. And beyond all these things put on love, which is the perfect bond of unity. And let the peace of Christ rule in your hearts, to which indeed you were called in one body; and be thankful. Let the word of Christ richly dwell within you, with all wisdom teaching and admonishing one another with psalms and hymns and spiritual songs, singing with thankfulness in your hearts to God. And whatever you do in word or deed, do all in the name of the Lord Jesus, giving thanks through Him to God the Father. *Col. 3:12–17*

. . . seeing that His divine power has granted to us everything pertaining to life and godliness, through the true knowledge of Him who called us by His own glory and excellence. For by these He has granted to us His precious and magnificent promises, in order that by them you might become partakers of the divine nature, having escaped the corruption that is in the world by lust. Now for this very reason also, applying all diligence, in your faith supply, moral excellence; and in your moral excellence, knowledge; and in your knowledge, self-control; and in your self-control, perseverance; and in your perseverance, godliness; and in your godliness, brotherly kindness; and in your brotherly kindness, Christian love. For if these qualities are yours and are increasing, they render you neither useless nor unfruitful in the true knowledge of our Lord Jesus Christ. For he who lacks these qualities is blind or short-sighted, having forgotten his purification from his former sins. Therefore, brethren, be all the more diligent to make certain about His calling and choosing you; for as long as you practice these things, you will never

stumble; for in this way the entrance into the eternal kingdom of our Lord and Savior Jesus Christ will be abundantly supplied to you.

2 Pet. 1:3–11

DENOUNCING AND DESCRIBING SIN

Now the deeds of the flesh are evident, which are: immorality, impurity, sensuality, idolatry, sorcery, enmities, strife, jealousy, outbursts of anger, disputes, dissensions, factions, envyings, drunkenness, carousings, and things like these, of which I forewarn you just as I have forewarned you that those who practice such things shall not inherit the kingdom of God.

Gal. 5:19–21

In reference to your former manner of life, you lay aside the old self, which is being corrupted in accordance with the lusts of deceit, and that you be renewed in the spirit of your mind, and put on the new self, which in the likeness of God has been created in righteousness and holiness of the truth.

Therefore, laying aside falsehood, speak truth, each one of you, with his neighbor, for we are members of one another. Be angry, and yet do not sin; do not let the sun go down on your anger, and do not give the devil an opportunity. Let him who steals steal no longer; but rather let him labor, performing with his own hands what is good, in order that he may have something to share with him who has need. Let no unwholesome word proceed from your mouth, but only such a word as is good for edification according to the need of the moment, that it may give grace to those who hear. And do not grieve the Holy Spirit of God, by whom you were sealed for the day of redemption. Let all bitterness and wrath and anger and clamor and slander be put away from you, along with all malice. And be kind to one another, tender-hearted, forgiving each other, just as God in Christ also has forgiven you. Therefore be imitators of God, as beloved children; and walk in love, just as Christ also loved you, and gave Himself up for us, an offering and a sacrifice to God as a fragrant aroma.

But do not let immorality or any impurity or greed even be named among you, as is proper among saints; and there must be no filthiness and silly talk, or coarse jesting, which are not fitting, but rather giving of thanks. For this you know with certainty, that no immoral or impure person or covetous man, who is an idolater, has an inheritance in the kingdom of Christ and God.   *Eph. 4:22–5:5*

CHAPTER EIGHT

CONFESSION: ACKNOWLEDGING OUR SIN TO GOD AND ANOTHER PERSON

CHRISTIAN PRINCIPLE: CONFESSION OF SIN	AA'S STEP FIVE	CHRISTIAN ADAPTATION
Therefore, confess your sins to one another, and pray for one another, so that you may be healed. *James 5:16*	Admitted to God, to ourselves, and to another human being the exact nature of our wrongs.	Confessed our sins to God and another person.

While in jail and waiting for his trial for assault charges, Steve sought God's forgiveness for his behavior. He began to experience Christ's mercy and presence in a new and powerful way. Steve consequently decided he would make God's will the directing force in his life.

This decision was quickly tested when Steve's lawyer advised him to plead innocent of his assault charge. By so doing, Steve would likely incur a lighter sentence. But Steve was guilty and he knew it. What was he to do? He sensed that God wanted him to acknowledge his crime in court. He took the matter to prayer and soon was convinced that, despite his lawyer's advice to the contrary, he must plead guilty because he was guilty.

Steve received a just and moderate sentence. But his time in jail could not restrict the incred-ible freedom he now experienced through obedience to God. Steve also learned the importance and freeing power of confession of sin—a lesson God desires all his children to learn.

A thorough self-examination brings us to a compelling question: What next? Now that we have explored sins' effect, what must we do to rid ourselves of its influence? How do we permit Jesus, our great physician, the opportunity to administer His "soul surgery" and systematically cut out the spiritual cancer of sin from our lives?

Confessing our sin is critical to the process of sanctification. It is the open, verbal expression to God and another person of our insights from our self-examination. Like the prodigal son returning to his father with a repentant attitude, we acknowledge with our heart and our lips that we have sinned with attention to detail.

Confession demands courage. Pride and fear cause us to question the need for this essential spiritual discipline. "Why must I tell my sins to another person? Why isn't God enough? God knows my sins, and He has already forgiven me." These challenges to confession are typical. Don't submit to them. Our ability to grow in Christ becomes immeasurably enhanced as we find the strength and humility to admit our sins to another person.

Old and New Testament verses alike make clear the importance of confession of sin.

> Speak to the sons of Israel, "When a man or woman commits any of the sins of mankind, acting unfaithfully against the Lord, and that person is guilty, then he shall confess his sins which he has committed, and he shall make restitution in full for his wrong, and add to it one-fifth of it, and give it to him whom he has wronged."[1]

> Therefore, confess your sins to one another, and pray for one another, so that you may be healed.[2]

The immediate impact of a thorough confession is often profound. We typically experience a sense of God's love and acceptance that we never understood before. God blesses our willingness to expose our sinful behavior with a repentant attitude.

Never approach confession with fear of God's punishment. God's forgiveness is not based on anything you do, including confessing of sin. It is instead based on what Jesus has done for you. God already knows your sin, and through Christ you have been forgiven. Confession provides us the opportunity to experience God's love and mercy in a unique and powerful way.

Be cautious not to approach confession as a routine and mechanical task. Confession is a serious spiritual exercise that must be approached with respect for God. Sin is serious, confession is serious, and God is serious. The confession of our sins to God should be serious as well.

It's good to be properly prepared. Six key areas of preparation are listed below.

1. Find the right listener.
2. Be prepared with central elements of Step Four.
3. Be prepared to include specifics and generalities.
4. Put aside enough time.
5. Pray before you begin.
6. Don't worry about doing a perfect confession.

Finding the right listener is important. Ideal listeners have a deep relationship with God, and you trust them. If you fear being judged, or suspect your listener will tell others about your sin, the honesty and openness you need will be hard to find. If you have sexually sensitive issues to confess, your listener should probably be the same sex as you.

Listeners' styles vary. Your listener might be interactive and provide input and direction. Your listener could be silent throughout your confession. Either style is effective. What's criti-

---

1. Num. 5:6–7
2. James 5:16

cal is your humble confession of sin before God and your listener.

Give yourself plenty of time. Two hours is a good starting point. Some people are more verbal then others. Some have had a longer or more sin-filled life. Take these things into consideration when you plan your confession, to avoid rushing through it. You can certainly schedule more than one confession if needed.

Be prepared with your written self-examination inventory. Reading your inventory line by line is not necessary, but highlighting elements that you think demand confession will help ensure that key issues are addressed.

Sinful behaviors or thoughts that provoke significant remorse or guilt should always be shared. Also, confess any pattern of habitual sin like sexual obsessions or chronic anger. These are issues that you will likely be addressing in more depth and detail as you grow in your Christian faith. It's important that you know yourself well.

Before starting your confession ask yourself the following:

- Do I understand that God through Christ has already forgiven me and this process is for the purging, not forgiveness, of sin?
- Have I selected a listener who understands this as well?
- Have I completed a thorough written self-examination?
- Have I organized myself well and determined what to confess?

Pray before you start. God is both a partner and a listener, so ask Him to guide you through the process. Ask for courage to be thorough and bring to mind things not yet written or understood.

Finally, don't worry about doing the perfect confession. Christ has already forgiven you, and the ongoing opportunities to confess missed sin will be available. Prayerfully, thoughtfully, and searchingly do the best you can, and God will bless your efforts.

CONFESSION WORKSHEET
FOR GROUP DISCUSSION AND PERSONAL REFLECTION

1. Consider the following Scripture and answer the questions.

He who conceals his transgressions will not prosper, But he who confesses and forsakes them will find compassion.

Prov. 28:13

Can you think of a time when you tried to conceal a transgression?
If so, list it. (List only a transgression you'd be willing to share with others.)

If so, what motivated you to do so?

Why else might we resist confessing our sin to another person?

Did any consequences result from your effort to conceal the above transgression? If so, what were they?

2. Based on the following scriptures, consider the benefit of confessed sin.

Therefore, confess your sins to one another, and pray for one another, so that you may be healed. The effective prayer of a righteous man can accomplish much.   *James 5:16*

If we confess our sins, He is faithful and righteous to forgive us our sins and to cleanse us from all unrighteousness.   *1 John 1:9*

CONFESSION WORKSHEET
FOR PERSONAL REFLECTION ONLY

In preparation of your confession, answer the following questions.

1. What fears do you have about confessing your sin?

2. List the sins that you feel the most shame or embarrassment for.

3. Have you committed any particular sins that you are uncomfortable confessing? If so list them below.

4. Whom would you be willing to complete your confession with?

5. List a date below as a time line for completing your confession.

SCRIPTURES RELATED TO CONFESSION OF SIN

So it shall be when he becomes guilty in one of these, that he shall confess that in which he has sinned. *Lev. 5:5*

Speak to the sons of Israel, "When a man or woman commits any of the sins of mankind, acting unfaithfully against the Lord, and that person is guilty, then he shall confess his sins which he has committed, and he shall make restitution in full for his wrong, and add to it one-fifth of it, and give it to him whom he has wronged." *Num. 5:6–7*

He who conceals his transgressions will not prosper, But he who confesses and forsakes them will find compassion. *Prov. 28:13*

And the son said to him, "Father, I have sinned against heaven and in your sight; I am no longer worthy to be called your son." *Luke 15:21*

Therefore, confess your sins to one another, and pray for one another, so that you may be healed. The effective prayer of a righteous man can accomplish much. *James 5:16*

If we confess our sins, He is faithful and righteous to forgive us our sins and to cleanse us from all unrighteousness. *1 John 1:9*

CHAPTER NINE

RESISTING TEMPTATION: OUR DETERMINATION NOT TO SIN

CHRISTIAN PRINCIPLE: RESISTING SIN	AA'S STEP SIX	CHRISTIAN ADAPTATION
No one who is born of God practices sin, because His seed abides in him; and he cannot sin, because he is born of God. *1 John 3:9*	Were entirely ready to have God remove all these defects of character.	Became determined to stop sinning.

Twice a week I try to defy time by playing basketball. One day, after my shower, I was about to place my sweaty laundry in a cloth gym bag. I hesitated, realizing that my gym bag would be better served if I first placed my clothes in a plastic bag. My bag seemed to cry out, "Please don't let those smelly, sweaty clothes touch me." But where was I to get a plastic bag?

A trash basket in the locker room suggested a possible solution. "Perhaps," I thought, "there are extra clean bags on the bottom of that basket." A quick investigation proved my theory correct.

As I proceeded to remove the bag, a piercing thought occurred to me: "Saul, that bag does not belong to you. You should return it." True, the bag didn't belong to me. I didn't pay for it, but my actions seemed justified. I countered with

"It's cheap. No one will miss it. Besides, I've contributed plenty to this health club." The voice replied, "It's not your bag. Return it!"

What was I to do? Should I listen to this annoying little voice that demanded I stay true to my values system, or take the convenient road of indefinitely borrowing this five-cent plastic bag?

This experience highlights a battle common to all Christians—the impulse to sin. As a Christian, I know stealing is wrong—yet I'm still tempted to steal. To live out my faith with integrity I must constantly put to death my impulse to sin. Yet without a strong conviction not to sin, I will certainly fail because the subtle influences that cause us to sin are powerful and pervasive.

Repentance, self-examination, and confession

provide us a firm foundation in the process of sanctification, but they are just a beginning. We cannot presume that by simply examining and confessing our sin, all is well, that resentments, pride, fits of anger, lust, materialism, gossiping, and selfish ambition will simply disappear; that God will instantly remove the desire to repeat these sins by virtue of our efforts.

The next element of sanctification is fought in the battleground of our mind—in our will. From this point on we must decide what will our attitude toward sin be. Do we view sin as a necessary evil that God will always graciously forgive, or are we determined no longer to tolerate sin in our day-to-day existence? Resisting asks the question: Are we willing to give up all of our sin?

Some might debate that complete removal of sin is impossible; that our corrupted human nature compels us to sin and therefore any consideration of sin's complete removal is foolish. This line of thought overlooks an incredible reality: Christians have the power not to sin.

As Christians, we have God's Spirit residing within us. His indwelling presence enables us to do what we could not do before—say no to sin. We are no longer powerless over lying because God gives us the ability not to lie. We are no longer powerless over slander because God gives us the power not to slander. We are no longer powerless over sexually immoral thoughts and behaviors because God gives us power over sinful thoughts and behaviors. *We are no longer powerless over sin.*

Paul states clearly that we are no longer slaves to sin, that we should consider ourselves dead to sin and that we should not let sin reign in our mortal bodies. He reminds us that we no longer are under an obligation to our flesh but to the Spirit. So by the Spirit we can put to death the deeds of the flesh.[1]

So now, through God's indwelling power, we have a choice. To sin or not to sin—that is the option. Daily we can choose to obey God despite the temptations we experience to sin. God through His Spirit has empowered us day by day, moment by moment to obey Him instead of our fleshly impulses.

Unfortunately, Christians often make the wrong choice. Frequently, we give ourselves permission to sin despite a God-given ability to resist. We justify our sin in a number of harmful ways.

We tolerate some sinful behaviors because they are pleasurable—our flesh enjoys them. They have provided us moments of delight and a sense of fulfillment that we have found rewarding and desirable. Sexual fantasies can be exciting, greed can provide a sense of security, and judgmental gossip can instill a sense of moral superiority. Consequently, despite the spiritual consequences, we might resist giving them up.

Sin can also have practical value. Angry outbursts are sin, yet they are often an effective way of manipulating other people to get what we want. Lying on taxes is sin, yet by doing so we might save some money.

But God condemns all sin, even those sins that we find pleasurable or practical. He requires that we become willing to give up all sin, even sins we enjoy—or that seem to work for us.

---

1. Rom. 8:11–14

These and other sins have ensured that our will would prevail in certain situations. Resisting sin demands that we trust in God alone, not in sin. We allow Him to meet all our needs, and we let go of sinful behaviors that have provided us with a false sense of power and security.

Abuse of God's grace is another justification to sin. God is in the grace business. He generously forgives us our sin and shows us mercy. This amazing grace is rightly emphasized within the Christian community. We can do nothing to earn it; Christ has done that through His death on the cross.

But grace can be twisted to become a license to sin. The faulty thinking goes something like this: "God loves me. His son died for my sins, and I'm forgiven. Therefore, if I sin, I'm automatically forgiven. Therefore, sin is not a problem. So I shall continue to sin without much concern and rest in God's merciful love. After all, He must forgive me."

Abuse of God's grace permits us to live in rebellion toward God. Paul condemns this dangerous deception when he asks the rhetorical question: "Are we to continue in sin that grace might increase?" His powerful and immediate response is: "May it never be!"[2]

As you consider resisting, you might ask yourself: Have I misused or abused God's grace? Have I used it as a license to sin, as opposed to an opportunity to repent of my sins? Have I used the often-quoted phrase "We are sinners saved by grace" to justify my indifference to sinful behavior that God has commanded me to refrain from?

Another justification to sin is fear of rejection—not by God, but by people. Some sinful behaviors unite us to people whose approval we desire. Consequently, we may be tempted to hold on to certain sins to maintain our relationship with these people.

As a new Christian, I was determined to give up all drug use. This decision put me at odds with most of my addicted friends. One day, while visiting an old friend, he lit a joint and handed it to me. It was his invitation to reestablish our friendship, which had been firmly cemented by this sinful behavior. Rejecting the joint would be both rejecting him and our fifteen-year friendship; accepting the joint would be sin. What was I to do? I was determined to follow God's will for my life, no matter the cost—and that relationship has never been the same.

Many people in this world embrace behaviors that God condemns. By rejecting sin, we put ourselves in conflict with this world and its sinful tendencies. Resisting sin demands that we ask ourselves some hard questions: Am I willing to live for God even if it requires changing relationships? Am I willing to live for God even if it means that some people might belittle me, misunderstand me, or judge me?

Christ's disciples must voluntarily surrender every prerogative we believe we have to sin, no matter how petty our sins appear or how comfortable they have become. No justification of sin is justified. Any rationalization to continue to sin is irrational. God makes clear that all willful sin will put us at odds with ourselves.

Sin may indeed be pleasurable for a season or

---

2. Rom. 6:1–2

may seem practical for a moment, but its eventual outcome is pain, hurt relationships, and spiritual death. As a loving Father, God desires to spare us the unpleasant consequences of sin. He warns us that we reap what we sow; if we sow to the flesh, we reap corruption; if we sow to the Spirit, we reap eternal life.[3]

The purposeful practice of any sin will always be destructive. It will alienate us from people, distance us from God, and destroy the peace that God promises.

Christ died for our sin. So why, in light of His incredible sacrifice, would we intentionally choose to do the very things over and over again that were responsible for His death? If we choose to live a sinful life, John suggests that our relationship with Christ may not truly exist.[4]

What then is your attitude toward sin? Do you view all sin as disobedience? Are you committed to reject all behaviors and attitudes that God has condemned?

3. Gal. 6:7–8
4. 1 John 3:8–9

RESISTING TEMPTATION WORKSHEET
FOR GROUP DISCUSSION AND PERSONAL REFLECTION

1. The verses below suggest that sin may have a passing pleasure. What are some reasons Christians might entertain or tolerate sin in their lives?

By faith Moses, when he had grown up, refused to be called the son of Pharaoh's daughter; choosing rather to endure ill-treatment with the people of God, than to enjoy the passing pleasures of sin.

Heb. 11:24–25

2. Read the following Scriptures and answer the questions. You might want to read all of Romans 6 to get a sense of context.

Now if we have died with Christ, we believe that we shall also live with Him, knowing that Christ, having been raised from the dead, is never to die again; death no longer is master over Him. For the death that He died, He died to sin, once for all; but the life that He lives, He lives to God. Even so consider yourselves to be dead to sin, but alive to God in Christ Jesus.

Therefore do not let sin reign in your mortal body that you should obey its lusts, and do not go on presenting the members of your body to sin as instruments of unrighteousness; but present yourselves to God as those alive from the dead, and your members as instruments of righteousness to God.

Rom. 6:8–13

But thanks be to God that though you were slaves of sin, you became obedient from the heart to that form of teaching to which you were committed, and having been freed from sin, you became slaves of righteousness. I am speaking in human terms because of the weakness of your flesh. For just as you presented your members as slaves to impurity and to lawlessness, resulting in further lawlessness, so now present your members as slaves to righteousness, resulting in sanctification. For when you were slaves of sin, you were free in regard to righteousness. Therefore what benefit were you then deriving from the things of which you are now ashamed? For the outcome of those things is death. But now having been freed from sin and enslaved to God, you derive your benefit, resulting in sanctification, and the outcome, eternal life. For the wages of sin is death, but the free gift of God is eternal life in Christ Jesus our Lord.

Rom. 6:17–23

What does Paul mean when he suggests that we consider ourselves "to be dead to sin"?

What does Paul mean when he states we should not allow sin to reign in our bodies?

What does Paul mean when he states we are freed from sin?

What does the term "slave to righteousness" mean?

What is the benefit of being enslaved to God?

3. **Read the following Scriptures and answer the questions.**

The one who practices sin is of the devil; for the devil has sinned from the beginning. The Son of God appeared for this purpose, that He might destroy the works of the devil. No one who is born of God practices sin, because His seed abides in him; and he cannot sin, because he is born of God. *1 John 3:8–9*

What does the phrase "practices sin" mean?

What was and is the purpose of the "Son of God"?

How does that purpose affect the Christian's attitude toward sin?

RESISTING TEMPTATION WORKSHEET
FOR PERSONAL REFLECTION ONLY

This worksheet is to help you analyze your attitude toward sin. Take the time prayerfully and conscientiously to evaluate your beliefs regarding the sins you have identified through the process of self-examination and confession. The first page is an example that you can follow for yourself.

If through this exercise you find that you lack determination or conviction to resist a certain sin, know that you can ask God for help. Consider adapting the below prayer to a particular sin that you may be resisting to give up.

Suggested Prayer for Willingness to Resist Sin

God, I know that Jesus died for my sins and that your will for my life is that I repent from the sinful behaviors you died for. I presently am struggling with the willingness to resist _____. Please instill within me the desire to stop this completely.

NAME OF SIN	WHAT, IF ANY, PURPOSE DID THIS SIN SERVE IN MY LIFE?	AM I DETERMINED TO RESIST THIS SIN?	IF NOT— WHY?
IDOLATRY My love of money	It allows me to feel superior to others who have less than I have, and enables me to feel independent of God or anyone else. It provides me with a false sense of security.	Yes—I want nothing to compete with my commitment to Christ.	
RESENT-MENT Of my parents	It allows me to feel morally superior to my parents. It reinforces my belief that they should be punished. It justifies my tendency to be angry.	Not sure	I'm not sure they deserve it.

Now in the left-hand columns, list the significant sins you've identified and complete this worksheet.

NAME OF SIN	WHAT, IF ANY, PURPOSE DID THIS SIN SERVE IN MY LIFE?	AM I DETERMINED TO RESIST THIS SIN?	IF NOT— WHY?

SCRIPTURES RELATED TO RESISTING SIN

THROUGH CHRIST WE HAVE THE POWER NOT TO SIN

And the slave does not remain in the house forever; the son does remain forever. If therefore the Son shall make you free, you shall be free indeed.
John 8:35–36

. . . knowing this, that our old self was crucified with Him, that our body of sin might be done away with, that we should no longer be slaves to sin; for he who has died is freed from sin.
Rom. 6:6–7

For the death that He died, He died to sin, once for all; but the life that He lives, He lives to God. Even so consider yourselves to be dead to sin, but alive to God in Christ Jesus.

Therefore do not let sin reign in your mortal body that you should obey its lusts, and do not go on presenting the members of your body to sin as instruments of unrighteousness; but present yourselves to God as those alive from the dead, and your members as instruments of righteousness to God. For sin shall not be master over you, for you are not under law, but under grace.

What then? Shall we sin because we are not under law but under grace? May it never be! Do you not know that when you present yourselves to someone as slaves for obedience, you are slaves of the one whom you obey, either of sin resulting in death, or of obedience resulting in righteousness? But thanks be to God that though you were slaves of sin, you became obedient from the heart to that form of teaching to which you were committed, and having been freed from sin, you became slaves of righteousness.
Rom. 6:10–18

But now having been freed from sin and enslaved to God, you derive your benefit, resulting in sanctification, and the outcome, eternal life. For the wages of sin is death, but the free gift of God is eternal life in Christ Jesus our Lord.
Rom. 6:22–23

For the law of the Spirit of life in Christ Jesus has set you free from the law of sin and of death. For what the Law could not do, weak as it was through the flesh, God did: sending His own Son in the likeness of sinful flesh and as an offering for sin, He condemned sin in the flesh, in order that the requirement of the Law might be fulfilled in us, who do not walk according to the flesh, but according to the Spirit.
Rom. 8:2–4

For you have not received a spirit of slavery leading to fear again, but you have received a spirit of adoption as sons by which we cry out, "Abba! Father!"
Rom. 8:15

My little children, I am writing these things to you that you may not sin. And if anyone sins, we have an Advocate with the Father, Jesus Christ the righteous.
1 John 2:1

Every one who practices sin also practices lawlessness; and sin is lawlessness. And you know that He appeared in order to take away sins; and in Him there is no sin.
1 John 3:4–5

The one who practices sin is of the devil; for the devil has sinned from the beginning. The Son of God appeared for this purpose, that He might destroy the works of the devil. No one who is born of God practices sin, because His seed abides in him; and he cannot sin, because he is born of God. *1 John 3:8–9*

If anyone sees his brother committing a sin not leading to death, he shall ask and God will for him give life to those who commit sin not leading to death. There is a sin leading to death; I do not say that he should make request for this. All unrighteousness is sin, and there is a sin not leading to death. *1 John 5:16–17*

CHAPTER TEN

PRUNING: ASKING GOD TO REMOVE OUR IMPULSE TO SIN

CHRISTIAN PRINCIPLE: PRUNING OF SIN	AA'S STEP SEVEN	CHRISTIAN ADAPTATION
Every branch in Me that does not bear fruit, He takes away; and every branch that bears fruit, He prunes it, that it may bear more fruit. *John 15:2*	Humbly asked Him to remove our shortcomings.	Asked God to remove our impulse to sin.

Before my conversion my speech was quite colorful. Using God's name in vain and cursing were hourly occurrences. After surrendering my life to Christ, I became increasingly aware of my need to change. God's word made clear that I had to honor God with my lips and avoid cursing and coarse joking.

At first the change was difficult. Years of habitual foul mouth had made this change a challenge. Initially I found myself saying things that I knew were wrong. I asked God for help. I asked Him to enable me to choose my words better. Change came slowly. I found myself cursing less, yet the impulse to curse still existed.

Within a few months a remarkable change had taken place—the impulse to curse had virtually left me. Not only was I not cursing, but I was rarely if ever being tempted to curse. Fueled by my willingness, God had performed spiritual surgery and removed the desire to curse. He had done for me what I could not do myself. He pruned my impulse to use foul language.

God is our source of change in the process of sanctification. He enables us to see our sin, detest our sin, desire its removal, and enable its removal. Only His power can change us. Only His indwelling presence can transform us into the image of Christ. For lack of a better word to describe God's role in the removal of sin, I am calling it *pruning*.

Pruning is simple. It's about prayer and power—our prayer and God's Power. We ask Him to eliminate the sinful behaviors and attitudes that have been habitual and hurtful. If we struggle with resentment, we beg Him to help us be forgiving. If we struggle with sexual fantasies, we ask Him to help us think only good and wholesome thoughts. If we struggle with gossip we ask that He fill our lips with loving kindness to the people in our lives. All along we do this, understanding that His power is the enabling source for our success in change.

God desires our prayers—yet some prayers appear to go unanswered. God's word has much to say about effective prayer.[1] Effective prayers are consistent with God's will. If we ask God for something that He has already determined is good for us we can feel confident of His blessings. In contrast, if I ask God for something that He knows will hurt me, I have no reason to expect my request will be honored.

Too often our prayers are selfish, prayed with little thought of how they fit into God's purpose for our lives. Such prayers have little likelihood of being granted. However, prayers consistent with God's purpose will always be granted because God is interested in blessing His children with things that He knows are good.

If my son asks for breakfast, as his father I am both happy and obligated to provide him food. If he asks for a handgun with bullets, I have no such obligation. Similarly, our Heavenly Father desires to give us good things. We should not hesitate to ask for those things that are biblically consistent with His will, nor should we doubt that He will provide them.

There is no doubt that God desires to prune sin from our lives. Christ died for our sins. He desires that we imitate His holiness. Surely God will honor our earnest and humble request to change, to become like Him in our thoughts and deeds. Prayers designed to achieve holiness will certainly be heard, particularly if we are sincere in our desire to change.

A helpful exercise is to ask God to individually remove every sinful habit noted in your self-examination. Our prayer should include not just focus on removal of the negative, but also on inserting the positive. Paul says we are no longer slaves to sin, that we should voluntarily become slaves to righteousness. With that idea in mind, we ask God to substitute our impulse to sin with an impulse to reflect His character. If you struggle with greed, ask God that you be satisfied with what you have and be generous with your possessions. If you tend to gossip, ask God to provide you words that strengthen others. Become clear about the attitudes and behaviors you want changed, and ask Him to change them.

---

1. See verses at the end of the chapter.

PRUNING WORKSHEET
FOR GROUP DISCUSSION AND PERSONAL REFLECTION

1. **Based on the following passages, what does Jesus mean when he says to "ask in My name"?**

And whatever you ask in My name, that will I do, that the Father may be glorified in the Son. If you ask Me anything in My name, I will do it.   *John 14:13–14*

2. **Based on the following passage, write the conditions of answered prayer.**

If you abide in Me, and My words abide in you, ask whatever you wish, and it shall be done for you.   *John 15:7*

And this is the confidence which we have before Him, that, if we ask anything according to His will, He hears us. And if we know that He hears us in whatever we ask, we know that we have the requests which we have asked from Him.   *1 John 5:14–15*

3. Based on the following passage, what is the purpose of answered prayer?

You did not choose Me, but I chose you, and appointed you, that you should go and bear fruit, and that your fruit should remain, that whatever you ask of the Father in My name, He may give to you.   *John 15:16*

PRUNING WORKSHEET
FOR PERSONAL REFLECTION AND APPLICATION

Complete the worksheet for each sin you've identified in the previous chapters. The worksheet will direct you to create a prayer asking God to remove the specific sin. The prayer should also include the new behavior that you hope will replace the old. If the sin is greed, ask God to make you generous and selfless. If the sin is slander, ask God to help you speak of others in kind and respectful ways. If you hate your father, ask God to help you love him and bless him. We thoughtfully request the desired behavior that will reflect a true conversion to God's will.

Then pray the prayer with meaning. If you are simply completing an exercise, yet in your heart you have no commitment to change, your prayer is inconsequential. God will never force His will or lifestyle on you. You must be willing to change.

Ask God for His aid in overcoming specific sinful behaviors you have struggled with. If you struggle with unforgiveness toward a specific person, ask God to help you love that person. If you struggle with unholy sexual behavior or thoughts, ask God to help you become pure in your actions and thoughts. Use these three steps to complete the worksheet.

1. List sin. Example: Gossip.
2. Create a prayer reflecting the change you would like to see based on God's word.
3. Pray the prayer and note the date prayed.

PRUNING PRAYER WORKSHEET

IDENTIFY SPECIFIC SIN	GOSSIPING, PARTICULARLY ABOUT MY EMPLOYER
Create a prayer asking God to remove the impulse to continue this sin and to substitute an element of Christian character.	Example: *God, I know I have been guilty of gossip. I ask that you help me have control of my words and from now on enable me to speak words that help others, not hurt them. Help me particularly speak kind words about my employer.*

NOTE THE DATE OF PRAYER: 3/17/2000

PRUNING PRAYER WORKSHEET

IDENTIFY SPECIFIC SIN	
Create a prayer asking God to remove the impulse to continue this sin and to substitute an element of Christian character.	

NOTE THE DATE OF PRAYER:

SCRIPTURES RELATED
TO PRUNING

PRAYER

And whatever you ask in My name, that will I do, that the Father may be glorified in the Son. If you ask Me anything in My name, I will do it. *John 14:13–14*

If you abide in Me, and My words abide in you, ask whatever you wish, and it shall be done for you. *John 15:7*

You did not choose Me, but I chose you, and appointed you, that you should go and bear fruit, and that your fruit should remain, that whatever you ask of the Father in My name, He may give to you. *John 15:16*

And in that day you will ask Me no question. Truly, truly, I say to you, if you shall ask the Father for anything, He will give it to you in My name. Until now you have asked for nothing in My name; ask, and you will receive, that your joy may be made full. *John 16:23–24*

In that day you will ask in My name; and I do not say to you that I will request the Father on your behalf. *John 16:26*

Whatever we ask we receive from Him, because we keep His commandments and do the things that are pleasing in His sight. *1 John 3:22*

And this is the confidence which we have before Him, that, if we ask anything according to His will, He hears us. And if we know that He hears us in whatever we ask, we know that we have the requests which we have asked from Him. *1 John 5:14–15*

GOD'S DESIRE THAT WE BE HOLY

Therefore you are to be perfect, as your heavenly Father is perfect. *Matt. 5:48*

To grant us that we, being delivered from the hand of our enemies, Might serve Him without fear, In holiness and righteousness before Him all our days. *Luke 1:74–75*

Abide in Me, and I in you. As the branch cannot bear fruit of itself, unless it abides in the vine, so neither can you, unless you abide in Me. I am the vine, you are the branches; he who abides in Me, and I in him, he bears much fruit; for apart from Me you can do nothing. *John 15:4–5*

Therefore, having these promises, beloved, let us cleanse ourselves from all defilement of flesh and spirit, perfecting holiness in the fear of God. *2 Cor. 7:1*

Therefore be imitators of God, as beloved children; and walk in love, just as Christ also loved you, and gave Himself up for us, an offering and a sacrifice to God as a fragrant aroma.

Eph. 5:1–2

Only conduct yourselves in a manner worthy of the gospel of Christ; so that whether I come and see you or remain absent, I may hear of you that you are standing firm in one spirit, with one mind striving together for the faith of the gospel. *Phil. 1:27*

Prove yourselves to be blameless and innocent, children of God above reproach in the midst of a crooked and perverse generation, among whom you appear as lights in the world, holding fast the word of life, so that in the day of Christ I may have cause to glory because I did not run in vain nor toil in vain. *Phil. 2:15–16*

For this is the will of God, your sanctification; that is, that you abstain from sexual immorality; that each of you know how to possess his own vessel in sanctification and honor, not in lustful passion, like the Gentiles who do not know God; and that no man transgress and defraud his brother in the matter because the Lord is the avenger in all these things, just as we also told you before and solemnly warned you. For God has not called us for the purpose of impurity, but in sanctification.   *1 Thess. 4:3–7*

For the grace of God has appeared, bringing salvation to all men, instructing us to deny ungodliness and worldly desires and to live sensibly, righteously and godly in the present age, looking for the blessed hope and the appearing of the glory of our great God and Savior, Christ Jesus; who gave Himself for us, that He might redeem us from every lawless deed and purify for Himself a people for His own possession, zealous for good deeds.   *Titus 2:11–14*

This is a trustworthy statement; and concerning these things I want you to speak confidently, so that those who have believed God may be careful to engage in good deeds. These things are good and profitable for men.   *Titus 3:8*

And let our people also learn to engage in good deeds to meet pressing needs, that they may not be unfruitful.   *Titus 3:14*

Pursue peace with all men, and the sanctification without which no one will see the Lord.   *Heb. 12:14*

But like the Holy One who called you, be holy yourselves also in all your behavior; because it is written, "You shall be holy, for I am holy."   *1 Pet. 1:15–16*

For by these He has granted to us His precious and magnificent promises, in order that by them you might become partakers of the divine nature, having escaped the corruption that is in the world by lust. Now for this very reason also, applying all diligence, in your faith supply moral excellence; and in your moral excellence, knowledge; and in your knowledge, self-control; and in your self-control, perseverance; and in your perseverance, godliness; and in your godliness, brotherly kindness; and in your brotherly kindness, Christian love. For if these qualities are yours and are increasing, they render you neither useless nor unfruitful in the true knowledge of our Lord Jesus Christ. For he who lacks these qualities is blind or short-sighted, having forgotten his purification from his former sins. Therefore, brethren, be all the more diligent to make certain about His calling and choosing you; for as long as you practice these things, you will never stumble.   *2 Pet. 1:4–10*

CHAPTER ELEVEN

RESTITUTION: RESTORING RELATIONSHIPS

CHRISTIAN PRINCIPLE: RESTITUTION	AA'S STEPS EIGHT AND NINE	CHRISTIAN ADAPTATION
Speak to the sons of Israel, "When a man or woman commits any of the sins of mankind, acting unfaithfully against the Lord, and that person is guilty, then he shall confess his sins which he has committed, and he shall make restitution in full for his wrong, and add to it one-fifth of it, and give it to him whom he has wronged." *Num. 5:6–7*	Made a list of all persons we had harmed, and became willing to make amends to them all. Made direct amends to such people wherever possible, except when to do so would injure them or others.	Made restitution for the harm our sin has done to others.

In 1983 I was preparing to return to New York for a visit, when an unexpected memory surfaced. I recalled that nine years earlier, as an active drug addict, I had stolen a tennis racket from a health club in New York City. "Why now?" I thought. "Why has this bothersome memory returned just prior to my short trip to New York?" The answer occurred to me swiftly: to make amends! God was encouraging me to make restitution for my past action.

I initially protested and tried to bargain with God. "It was so long ago, plus my trip is too short to add any new inconvenient plans." I assured Him that if it were convenient, I would make amends.

God has an interesting sense of humor. Immediately upon my arrival in New York, my father suggested that we spend the afternoon visiting the South Street Seaport in Manhattan. Coincidentally, the South Street Seaport was one short block from the health club where I had stolen the tennis racket.

My lame excuse was immediately replaced with the clear awareness that God wanted me to make amends, so I did. Despite resistance from my father, who assured me I'd end up involuntarily admitted to a psych ward, I went to the club and confessed to a sin and a crime that I had committed nine years earlier. My goal was to make things right and obey God.

In the presence of two employees and the tennis club manager, I confessed my history of addiction, theft, and my desire to make restitution. The manager of the tennis club not only received my amend but also, in the presence of my father, offered me a job in the club. Imagine that. I confess to criminal behavior, and the one I offended offers to employ me. God certainly has a sense of humor.

As followers of Christ we are called to be at peace with everyone, as much as possible. This goal cannot be accomplished without the willingness to admit and respond to the harm our sin has caused others. Our effort to amend sin's harm is restitution.

Jesus proclaims the importance of restitution when He states: "First be reconciled to your brother"[1] before you come to God. From God's perspective it's difficult to separate our relationship with Him from our relationship with others. Ignoring our sin's impact on others will always distance us from God.

The conversion of Zaccheus powerfully illustrates the principle of restitution in the New Testament. Zaccheus was a wealthy chief tax collector who had likely abused his power by overtaxing the people of Israel for his own personal gain. As a thief and a backsliding Jew, Zaccheus was an unlikely candidate for a visit from the Messiah. Nonetheless, Jesus sought Zaccheus out, called him by name, and asked to stay at his house.

Contact with Jesus radically changed Zaccheus from a thief to a philanthropist. Immediately Zaccheus proclaimed his intent to make restitution for the harm he had done to others. He didn't just say: "I'm sorry I stole." He didn't just assure Jesus that he would personally apologize for his actions. No, Zaccheus promised to give half his possessions to the poor and pay back four times the amount to anyone he had defrauded.

Christ was pleased with this response. Zaccheus's willingness to restore the stolen money reflected a deeply felt conviction to live his life for God, not himself. By virtue of this heartfelt decision to change, Jesus proclaimed that Zaccheus had become a "son of Abraham." Abraham's obedience to God characterized his life. As Zaccheus demonstrated obedience to God, He became a "son of Abraham." God requires from us the same obedience.

Restitution is mentioned in the Bible but is rarely encouraged in Christian practice. God is pleased when we, too, are willing to take responsibility for the harm our sin has done to others.

Self-serving rationalizations will often resist restitution. Our minds cling to thoughts like: "I don't need to make amends because God has already forgiven me" or ". . . because he hurt me worse than I hurt him" or ". . . because I know other Christians who have never made amends." These rationalizations attempt to justify our sin and only distance us from God and others.

Restitution provides us freedom. Fear and guilt will haunt those who indifferently offend others. This indifference will certainly contribute to a growing distance between God and the sinner. Conversely, restoring relationships through restitution enables us to live at peace with all whenever possible.

Restitution also witnesses God's power to others. Truly changed lives are difficult to account for. Zaccheus changed, and his willingness to pay back those he had stolen from confirmed that change. How were people to account for such a change? Zaccheus's uncharacteristic generosity could certainly cause some observers to

---

1. Matt. 5:23–24

conclude that God was real. Similarly, God's power in our lives can become evident to others as we obey His command to make restitution.

Beware of pride as a deterrent to making amends. People we have hurt have often hurt us. Our pride might demand that we withhold amends until they make the first move. After all, we confidently assert, "their sin is far larger than ours." Yet God requires that we take responsibility for our own sin despite what others have done to us.

Fear can also deter restitution. Fear of financial insecurity, fear of the offended party's response, and fear of a damaged reputation are some reasons why we might hesitate to follow through with making amends. It's true that unpleasant consequences might result from making amends. However, more typically we are respected and sometimes rewarded for our efforts in taking responsibility for our sinful behaviors.

As we confront these fears, we should always be mindful of two things: First, our God is powerful and loving. If He is guiding us in this process, He will assure the outcome as beneficial. That does not guarantee that we will always be comfortable with restitution's immediate consequences. Depending on the sin, we may lose a friend, have less cash, lose a job, or perhaps go to jail. Second, we can be assured that if we are following Christ's will, He will cause "all things to work together for good."[2]

The process of restitution involves four simple steps:

1. Make a list of people you have sinned against.

2. Determine the effect of your sin.
3. Determine the best way to make restitution.
4. Make restitution.

Making the list is easy. Review your self-examination inventory. It should already include the names of individuals or organizations you have sinned against. If you stole money from your employer, your employer should be on the list. If you lied to your spouse, your spouse should be on the list.

But don't stop there. If you had difficulty with slander or gossip think about whom these sinful tendencies have affected. If you are subject to angry outbursts, add the people whom your anger has victimized. Be as comprehensive as possible and keep in mind that the purpose of this spiritual exercise is not to beat yourself up, but rather to deal with the effect your sin has had on others.

Next, consider the effect of that sin on the individual or agency you sinned against. Understanding sin's impact provides practical guidance regarding the type of restitution required. It also acts as deterrent against future sin. If I have lied about a co-worker to enhance my chances for a promotion, I have slandered my co-worker. What effect has that slander had on my co-worker's reputation? If I verbally abuse my children, I ask myself how has this affected them. These questions enable you rightly to see how to proceed with your amends.

Now consider what would be the fair and best way to make amends. Amends should reflect the impact of your sin. Apologies are good and necessary but are often inadequate to right the wrongs committed. They typically must be

---

2. Rom. 8:28

accompanied by new behaviors that reflect true repentance. If I apologize to my employer for routinely coming in late to work, yet I continue with the same behavior, my restitution is false.

Restitution requires prayerful wisdom and, occasionally, direction from others. If making direct amends has the potential to harm others, we must carefully and prayerfully consider the best way to approach it. If I have been sexually unfaithful to my spouse or perhaps struggle with pornography or sexual fantasies, the difficult question is whether to tell my spouse. Would admitting such behavior hurt my spouse further? Would the best amend be to repent of my sin and be accountable to someone else for my change?

There is no simple rule one can apply to this situation. I suspect that God will lead some people to make direct amends to the person offended, and others might be led to amend the behavior in a less direct manner. Such questions should be considered prayerfully and carefully.

As you consider your list, you will likely find some amends easier to make than others. You may feel tremendous conviction to make restitution for a particular sin; certainly start there.

You may have sinned against friends and family who will support you despite your offense. Making amends to them will likely be easier.

However, some amends will appear more touchy, having the potential for embarrassment or possibly unpleasant consequences. Do not let your fears prevent you from following through. Ask God to give you wisdom and courage to proceed with your restitution.

Some of those offended might be deceased or unavailable. In such cases, prayerfully consider if anything can or should be done with the family of the individuals involved. Perhaps nothing else is needed but the willingness not to repeat the sin.

The time frame of restitution depends on the size of your list, the availability of those offended, and your willingness to follow through. Look your list over and ask yourself: How long should it take me to address this list? Then set yourself a reasonable goal of completion. Perhaps you could highlight certain amends that you feel take priority and address them first, then continue on to those amends that seem less time-sensitive.

RESTITUTION WORKSHEET
FOR GROUP DISCUSSION AND PERSONAL REFLECTION

Speak to the sons of Israel, "When a man or woman commits any of the sins of mankind, acting unfaithfully against the Lord, and that person is guilty, then he shall confess his sins which he has committed, and he shall make restitution in full for his wrong, and add to it one-fifth of it, and give it to him whom he has wronged. But if the man has no relative to whom restitution may be made for the wrong, the restitution which is made for the wrong must go to the Lord for the priest, besides the ram of atonement, by which atonement is made for him." *Num. 5:6–8*

1. Read the above passage and answer the following questions.

When we sin against someone, how many parties have been offended?

How would our relationship with God be affected if we choose not to restore damage we've done to others?

2. Has anyone you know offended you and later attempted to make restitution? What happened?

3. How did those efforts to make restitution affect your relationship with that person?

4. What excuses might we have to justify not making amends to people we have offended?

RESTITUTION WORKSHEET
FOR PERSONAL REFLECTION ONLY

Referring back to your self-examination inventory, list the people you have harmed and complete the following worksheet. Look first at the sample worksheet.

SAMPLE RESTITUTION WORKSHEET

Person or group I sinned against	Nature and effect of my sin	Type of restitution required ·	Am I willing to make amends? If not why?	Date restitution made.
My employer	Stole: I would leave work early and arrive late and get paid for a full day.	Apology to employer, and improved work habits.	Yes	3/19
My father	Bitter resentment over past hurts. Would often slander him to others.	Ask father for forgiveness, speak respectfully to others about my father.	I'm not sure. I feel I'm too angry to take responsibility for my behavior.	

Person or group I sinned against	Nature and effect of my sin	Type of restitution required	Am I willing to make amends? If not why?	Date restitution made.

SCRIPTURES RELATED TO RESTITUTION

And the one who takes the life of an animal shall make it good, life for life. *Lev. 24:18*

Speak to the sons of Israel, "When a man or woman commits any of the sins of mankind, acting unfaithfully against the Lord, and that person is guilty, then he shall confess his sins which he has committed, and he shall make restitution in full for his wrong, and add to it one-fifth of it, and give it to him whom he has wronged. But if the man has no relative to whom restitution may be made for the wrong, the restitution which is made for the wrong must go to the Lord for the priest, besides the ram of atonement, by which atonement is made for him." *Num. 5:6–8*

If a wicked man restores a pledge, pays back what he has taken by robbery, walks by the statutes which ensure life without committing iniquity, he will surely live; he shall not die. *Ezek. 33:15*

If therefore you are presenting your offering at the altar, and there remember that your brother has something against you, leave your offering there before the altar, and go your way; first be reconciled to your brother, and then come and present your offering. *Matt. 5:23–24*

And He entered and was passing through Jericho. And behold, there was a man called by the name of Zaccheus; and he was a chief tax-gatherer, and he was rich. And he was trying to see who Jesus was, and he was unable because of the crowd, for he was small in stature. And he ran on ahead and climbed up into a sycamore tree in order to see Him, for He was about to pass through that way. And when Jesus came to the place, He looked up and said to him, "Zaccheus, hurry and come down, for today I must stay at your house." And he hurried and came down, and received Him gladly. And when they saw it, they all began to grumble, saying, "He has gone to be the guest of a man who is a sinner." And Zaccheus stopped and said to the Lord, "Behold, Lord, half of my possessions I will give to the poor, and if I have defrauded anyone of anything, I will give back four times as much." And Jesus said to him, "Today salvation has come to this house, because he, too, is a son of Abraham. For the Son of Man has come to seek and to save that which was lost." *Luke 19:1–10*

Never pay back evil for evil to anyone. Respect what is right in the sight of all men. If possible, so far as it depends on you, be at peace with all men. *Rom. 12:17–18*

Render to all what is due them: tax to whom tax is due; custom to whom custom; fear to whom fear; honor to whom honor. *Rom. 13:7–10*

CHAPTER TWELVE

DAILY SANCTIFICATION: RESISTING SIN DAILY

CHRISTIAN PRINCIPLE: DAILY SANCTIFICATION	AA'S STEP TEN	CHRISTIAN ADAPTATION
And He was saying to them all, "If anyone wishes to come after Me, let him deny himself, and take up his cross daily, and follow Me." *Luke 9:23* For we who live are constantly being delivered over to death for Jesus' sake, that the life of Jesus also may be manifested in our mortal flesh. *2 Cor. 4:11*	Continued to take personal inventory and when we were wrong promptly admitted it.	Daily resist the temptation to sin, and if we sin we immediately confess it to God and make restitution to those affected.

It was a beautiful summer evening. The air was dry, the sun was setting, and an enjoyable soccer game had just concluded. My son's team had tied their township rivals. Now it was time to go home, but my son, Daniel, was back on the soccer field playing one-on-one with a friend. I yelled out, "Daniel, whose ball is that?" "The coach's," he replied as they continued to play. I noticed the coach preparing to leave, so I yelled, "Give the ball back to the coach and let's go home." Daniel appeared to ignore this command, so I repeated it with a bit more oomph: "Daniel, bring the ball to the coach, we need to go home." Daniel replied, "I didn't take the ball. Tim did. He needs to bring the ball back."

Now I was upset. Daniel had ignored my first request and was now defying my second. I was in a hurry to leave, I didn't want to inconve-

nience the coach, and I expected my son to listen to me. With an angry scowl on my face, I sternly blurted out, "Bring the ball back now!"

I was immediately convicted of sin. My angry response was wrong. It violated God's will for my life and offended my son. At first I tried to justify my actions: "If he had only listened to me the first or second time, I would not have needed to be so stern." But I knew deep in my heart that I had sinned, and I had to deal with it. When I eventually found the humility to acknowledge my sin, I asked God and Daniel for forgiveness.

Why did this happen? Why after twenty years of Christian life do I still struggle with anger and other temptations to sin?

The answer is simple—I am not yet perfect. As a believer, I strive for perfection, to be like Christ in all I do and say, to be completely sinless in my words and deeds—yet at times I fail. Or might I suggest that at times we all fail.

It's not because we must sin. God has provided us His power, His Spirit, to keep us from sinning. Yet sanctification is a lifelong process.

The maintenance of our revived spiritual state through the practice of repentance, self-examination, confession, and restitution can be accomplished only through reinforcing these ideals day by day. Our daily effort not to sin and to reflect Christ's character is daily sanctification.

Daily sanctification requires that each day we review our behaviors and actions, examining them in the light of God's commands. Daily we are on the lookout for sin in our lives and attempt to cut off its ugly head before it surfaces. If we fall short, if we err, if we sin, we address it immediately, keeping short accounts with God and the people whom our sinful behavior may have affected.

Why daily, you ask? Why must we constantly focus on our sins? Might this be a morbid distraction leading to depression? No, not if our focus is on Christ. If we daily seek to please God and live for Him, we also must die for Him. Not physical death, but death of self. Each day we choose to put aside our will and replace it with His. Each day we crucify our flesh and say no to its lusts. Daily we give God's indwelling presence the green light to be the guiding force for our thoughts and behaviors. Daily we die to self and carry our own cross in tribute to the merciful God who called us into this dynamic partnership. As Jesus challenged us to daily deny ourselves, we obey.[1] As Paul proclaimed "I die daily," so we choose to do the same.[2]

Daily sanctification, when applied correctly, ensures that we "may not sin." We take preventive measures to ensure that we reject whatever temptation comes our way.

Preventive intervention in the process of daily sanctification is aided by understanding the relationship between temptations and sin. Our flesh, or sinful impulses, often tempts us to sin. But the temptation to sin is not sin itself. Submitting to the temptation and actually following through with it—that is sin. In order not to sin, I must, with God's help, be willing to say no to my sinful lusts before they bear fruit. Let's consider a number of examples that illustrate this process.

- A cashier mistakenly gives me a twenty-dollar bill in change instead of a five when I pay for a meal. I immediately realize that I can walk out of the restaurant richer than when I arrive. My lust for money tempts me by shouting: "Keep it, no one will ever know!" That voice is not sin, but it's tempting me to sin. If I listen to it and do what it says, then I have sinned.

- While playing with his yo-yo, my son puts a hole in my newly painted wall. I have told him at least three times that I want him to do his yo-yo tricks outside. A voice within me says: "Hit him so he learns never to do that again." This voice is tempting me to sin, but it is not sin. If I submit to the temptation, then I sin.

---

1. Luke 9:23
2. 1 Cor. 15:31

- While flipping channels on TV, I pause at a station featuring a barely dressed women. A voice within me suggests, "Let's watch this show and let your imagination run wild." That temptation is not sin, but if I obey it, I sin.

- While at church you become aware of a family with a significant financial need. You sense God directing you to provide some financial support, but a voice within you says, "They should learn to manage on their own. After all, you did." The temptation to withhold financial assistance is not sin, but obeyed, it becomes sin. "Therefore, to one who knows the right thing to do, and does not do it, to him it is sin."3

I once heard Billy Graham say, "You can't keep a sparrow from flying above your head, but you can prevent it from constructing a nest on your hair." Similarly, while in this earthly body, we will invariably be tempted to sin, but we need not succumb to the temptation. God's indwelling presence will "convict the world concerning sin"4 as well as the temptation to sin, and then give us the power to resist it. Our responsibility is to be as sensitive and obedient as possible to God's voice within us.

Our initial self-examination has likely revealed that certain temptations have been prevalent. We should monitor these areas of weakness regularly. Daily we ask how we're doing with that particular temptation. If anger has been a significant issue, we ask, "Have I been tempted to angrily overreact?" If pride, materialism, or gossip are our issues, we consider, "Have they surfaced today? If so how did I respond?"

Again, our goal is not to sin, but if we do sin, we promptly repent and make restitution to the offended party or parties. Sin always impacts God, so repentance always asks for His forgiveness. We can be assured of God's forgiveness because, "If we confess our sins, He is faithful and righteous to forgive us our sins."5 Godly repentance of any sin always includes the honest desire not to repeat the sinful behavior.

If our sin touches others, we must consider what action, or restitution, should follow. Do I apologize for my behavior, ask forgiveness, or somehow bless the person I have offended?

Daily sanctification keeps us intimately close to our source of life. Conversely, unrepentant sin will always distance us from God. The longer we grieve God's Spirit, the harder our heart becomes. The harder our heart becomes, the more difficult it is to repent. It's essential that we deal with sin immediately to prevent a spiritual crust from forming over our heart.

As we apply daily sanctification, something wonderful happens—we begin to change. Increasingly our character reflects Christ's indwelling presence. Our impulse toward particular sins begins to fade away and is replaced with self-control previously unavailable to us. Our pruning prayer becomes a practical reality in our lives.

3. James 4:17
4. John 16:8
5. 1 John 1:9

DAILY SANCTIFICATION WORKSHEET
FOR GROUP DISCUSSION AND PERSONAL REFLECTION

1. **Read the following Scripture and answer the questions.**

Let no one say when he is tempted, "I am being tempted by God"; for God cannot be tempted by evil, and He Himself does not tempt anyone. But each one is tempted when he is carried away and enticed by his own lust. Then when lust has conceived, it gives birth to sin; and when sin is accomplished, it brings forth death.

James 1:13–15

Where does temptation to sin come from?

What does the term "carried away" mean?

What is meant by lust conceiving something?

What is the outcome of sin?

2. **Based on the following Scripture, answer the questions.**

No temptation has overtaken you but such as is common to man; and God is faithful, who will not allow you to be tempted beyond what you are able, but with the temptation will provide the way of escape also, that you may be able to endure it.

1 Cor. 10:13

What role does God play in our resisting temptation?

What does Paul mean by a "way of escape"?

Describe three circumstances when you were tempted to sin,
but God provided you a way of escape.

Will God continue to provide us a way of escape if we daily resist sin?

DAILY SANCTIFICATION WORKSHEET
FOR PERSONAL REFLECTION ONLY

The following lists are designed for your daily review. Each day put aside some time prayerfully to consider if you have sinned and if you exhibited Christ's character. The worksheet guides you into a godly response if you did sin.

DAILY REVIEW OF CHRIST'S CHARACTER IN MY LIFE

CHARACTER TRAIT	DID I EXHIBIT THIS TODAY?	DID I MISS AN OPPORTUNITY TO DO SO?	IS THERE SOMETHING I LEFT UNDONE THAT I NEED TO DO?
Forgiveness			
Compassion and Mercy			
Humility			
Kindness			
Patience and Long-suffering			
Hope			
Love			
Peace			
Gentleness			
Self-Control			
Joy			

DAILY REVIEW OF SIN IN MY LIFE

TYPE OF SIN	DID I COMMIT THIS SIN?	IF SO, HOW MUST I ADDRESS IT WITH GOD?	IF SO, HOW MUST I ADDRESS IT WITH OTHERS?
Idolatry			
Prejudice or Partiality			
Pride			
Sexual Lust			
Hoarding or Materialism			
Resentment or Bitterness			
Selfishness			
Envy			
Guile or Deceit			
Malice			
Stealing			
Greed or Coveting			
Anxiety or Fear			

DAILY REVIEW OF SIN IN MY LIFE (continued)

TYPE OF SIN	DID I COMMIT THIS SIN?	IF SO, HOW MUST I ADDRESS IT WITH GOD?	IF SO, HOW MUST I ADDRESS IT WITH OTHERS?
Slander or Gossip			
Lying or Deception			
Complaining			
Cursing and Using God's Name in Vain			
Coarse Joking or Vulgarity			

SCRIPTURE RELATED TO DAILY SANCTIFICATION

How many are my iniquities and sins? Make known to me my rebellion and my sin.

Job 13:23

Tremble, and do not sin; Meditate in your heart upon your bed, and be still. *Ps. 4:4*

Who can discern his errors? Acquit me of hidden faults. *Ps. 19:12*

Examine me, O Lord, and try me; Test my mind and my heart. *Ps. 26:2*

I will remember my song in the night; I will meditate with my heart; And my spirit ponders.

Ps. 77:6

I considered my ways, And turned my feet to Thy testimonies. *Ps. 119:59*

Search me, O God, and know my heart; Try me and know my anxious thoughts; And see if there be any hurtful way in me, And lead me in the everlasting way. *Ps. 139:23–24*

The heart is more deceitful than all else and is desperately sick; Who can understand it?

Jer. 17:9

Let us examine and probe our ways, And let us return to the Lord. *Lam. 3:40*

Thus says the Lord of hosts, "Consider your ways!" *Hag. 1:7*

Therefore whoever eats the bread or drinks the cup of the Lord in an unworthy manner, shall be guilty of the body and the blood of the Lord. But let a man examine himself, and so let him eat of the bread and drink of the cup.

1 Cor. 11:27–28

But if we judged ourselves rightly, we should not be judged. *1 Cor. 11:31*

Test yourselves to see if you are in the faith; examine yourselves! Or do you not recognize this about yourselves, that Jesus Christ is in you—unless indeed you fail the test?

2 Cor. 13:5

For if anyone thinks he is something when he is nothing, he deceives himself. But let each one examine his own work, and then he will have reason for boasting in regard to himself alone, and not in regard to another. For each one shall bear his own load. *Gal. 6:3–5*

CHAPTER THIRTEEN

ABIDING: DAILY SEEKING AND SUBMITTING TO CHRIST'S WILL

CHRISTIAN PRINCIPLE: ABIDING	AA'S STEP ELEVEN	CHRISTIAN ADAPTATION
Abide in Me, and I in you. As the branch cannot bear fruit of itself, unless it abides in the vine, so neither can you, unless you abide in Me. I am the vine, you are the branches; he who abides in Me, and I in him, he bears much fruit; for apart from Me you can do nothing. *John 15:4–5*	Sought through prayer and meditation to improve our conscious contact with God *as we understood Him,* praying only for knowledge of His will for us and the power to carry that out.	Daily seek and submit to Christ's will through prayer, meditation, bible study, and obedience.

Mission Impossible was a classic TV program from the 1960s. Each weekly show would start with Mr. Phelps receiving audiotaped instructions about a secret mission that the government wanted his group of skilled experts to accomplish. The instructions would always end with the statement, "If you choose to accept this mission, the secretary will disavow any knowledge of it," and then the tape would self-destruct. Of course, Mr. Phelps's team always accepted and accomplished the mission.

As Christians we, too, are asked to accomplish an impossible mission. But our requester is not the government, and the means of communication is not an audiotape. Our mission comes from God and is communicated by His Spirit. The general nature of our mission is clear—to represent Jesus. But the specific nature of our mission on a daily basis is not always clear or easy. Unlike Mr. Phelps, whose contact with his instructor was occasional, ours must be daily.

God has a plan for our lives. Certain elements of that plan are obvious. We know that we are not to sin. We know that we are to love. We know that we are to become more and more like Christ Himself. But the daily application of that plan requires wisdom and direction and power that can come only from God Himself. Daily we must seek God's face for the direction and power to accomplish His will. Each day we must talk to Him, listen to Him, and obey Him. Each day we Christians must proactively seek God's will to live out God's purpose in our life.

Our daily effort to connect with Christ and

seek His power and direction is called "abiding." Jesus says that if we abide in Him, we will bear much fruit.[1] So abide we must, and we do so through a number of daily disciplines.

Abiding begins with prayer. Daily we ask God: "What would you have me do today? How can I best serve you today?" Our request is purposeful, reflecting a humble ignorance of God's plan and a burning desire for insight and understanding. We desire to make ourselves available to live out whatever purpose He determines for us that day.

Too often Christians consider God to be their personal servant, a divine genie at their beck and call. God's role, they presume, is to bless the plans they have already made for their lives. They ask God to give them something or permit something to happen. And if it doesn't they become hurt and angry and convinced that God is indifferent or doesn't love them.

James speaks to this warped tendency and its ineffectiveness. He says, "You ask and do not receive, because you ask with wrong motives, so that you may spend it on your own pleasures."[2] God requires from His people an attitude of humility. If we pray selfishly, we can expect few results; but if we pray for things that we already know God desires to give us, we can expect great results.

> If you abide in Me, and My words abide in you, ask whatever you wish, and it shall be done for you.[3]

Abiding includes reflection, or meditation, on God's word. We can ask Jesus for whatever we wish and expect to receive it—as long as our request matches His will and word. The more familiar we become with His words, the better we understand their purpose and directives. Consequently, the more effective our prayers. Why? Because God is pleased to fulfill His will in our lives. We can confidently ask for the things that we know God desires. By daily reflecting on His word, we learn His will for our lives.

Which of these two prayers is more consistent with God's will: "God, help me love my enemy" or "God, please give me a BMW"? It's safe to say that asking for a BMW is more of a long shot. God's word says nothing to assure my entitlement to a luxury car, but I am absolutely sure He wants me to love my enemies because He has commanded me to do so.[4] So, the more familiar we become with God's will through knowledge of His word, the more effective our prayers.

Abiding includes seeking direction. As believers, we can learn from God's indwelling presence. Consider John's words:

> And as for you, the anointing which you received from Him abides in you, and you have no need for anyone to teach you; but as His anointing teaches you about all things, and is true and is not a lie, and just as it has taught you, you abide in Him.[5]

Because God abides or lives within, He can

---

1. John 15:5
2. James 4:3
3. John 15:7
4. Matt. 5:44
5. 1 John 2:27

reveal His will to you. His abiding presence helps us to understand His word and apply it to our lives.

Daily we read the Bible and then ask God that His understanding of His Words become our understanding. As I read "love thy neighbor," I ask what this means to me. Who is my neighbor? What does love mean in this context, and how am I to apply this in my day-to-day life? This type of reflection will enable God to open our hearts and minds to His will for our lives.

The Bible is often silent regarding the specific details of numerous choices we face daily. Should I find a new job? Should I buy a new car? Should I go to a certain church? Should I date or marry a particular person?

But God is not silent, nor is He indifferent. We can be confident that He is able and willing to direct us in the day-to-day operation of our lives—if we desire to know and apply His will. In such cases we petition God for guidance and direction and reflectively wait for an answer. Daily we must ask God, "What is your will for me this day?" Then we open our heart to His direction.

Abiding requires patience. Hearing God's voice and direction demands that we spend quality time with Him. A life crammed with activities, even wholesome godly activities, will make such communion difficult, if not impossible. Daily we must put aside time to pray, reflect on Scripture, and open our heart to God's directions. Like Jesus, we regularly seek solitude to commune with our Heavenly Father. Those times empower us to proceed in our mission with more clarity and power.

Abiding's purpose is not just to understand God's will, but also to obey it. This may sound obvious, but it's safe to say that God will require us to do things that we find difficult or unpleasant. Our flesh might initially recoil from His commands. His standards are high. His ways are different from ours. Invariably we should expect conflicts between our will and His. When aware of such conflict, we must choose His will, despite our resistance.

What might we resist? Perhaps you've had a conflict with your spouse. While spending time reading God's word, His Spirit challenges you to ask for forgiveness and apologize for your actions. Your stubborn pride immediately resists. It shouts, "No." It assures you that you were the one wronged, you deserve the apology. The logical response is to inflict pain equal to your suffering. Expect this to happen. At times you will be tempted to resist God's will, but you need not submit to this resistance. God will empower you to obey—if you're willing.

God's power for obedience is dramatically illustrated by the last words of the martyr Stephen. He is a dynamic example of God's power working through a mere human willing to be obedient—no matter the cost. God provided Stephen the opportunity to proclaim Christ's love to others. His message was not well received. In fact, it provoked an angry response that ultimately led his listeners to stone him to death.

Yet what was Stephen's response? Did he insist that God avenge him? Did Stephen demand their blood for his own? Did he curse God for allowing this event? No! His dying words were "Lord, do not hold this sin against them."[6]

---

6. Acts 7:59–60

Words reminiscent of Christ's words while dying on the cross: "Father, forgive them; for they do not know what they are doing."[7]

Where does this power come from? Where can mere humans find the strength to proclaim their faith despite the threat of death? By what power can humans find the strength to forgive their murderer? The answer is clear—from God, and God alone—but such power is available to us only if we abide in Him.

His abiding strength will enable us to accomplish all He directs us to do. We may be weak and proud and resistant, but He is strong, powerful, and able. Whatever changes He requires, whatever requests He makes, whatever directives He commands, He also provides the resources to accomplish His will.

If we lack the will or faith to obey Him, we can ask for more. "God, help me love my spouse more. God, help me to forgive my father for his hurtful behavior. God, help me be a better employee. God, give me the willingness to overcome my addictive behavior." Freely, we should ask for His strength to accomplish His will. Confidently we can assume He will provide it, and more. His will is for us to do His will. His delight is our obedience. His desire is for us to proclaim with the Apostle Paul's assurance: "I can do all things through Him who strengthens me."[8]

As you consider the daily application of abiding, you might ask yourself the following questions:

- How much time should I daily put aside for prayer and meditation?
- When is the best time to do so?
- Where is the best place to do so?

I would suggest no less than thirty minutes daily. Also select a time and place that will provide you peace from this world's distractions and promote an alert mind. Begin today if possible.

---

7. Luke 23:34
8. Phil. 4:13

ABIDING WORKSHEET
FOR GROUP DISCUSSION AND PERSONAL REFLECTION

Jesus therefore was saying to those Jews who had believed Him, "If you abide in My word, then you are truly disciples of Mine; and you shall know the truth, and the truth shall make you free."

John 8:31–32

1. **What does abiding in Jesus' word mean?**

2. **Based on the following Scripture, what is the outcome of abiding in Jesus' word?**

Abide in Me, and I in you. As the branch cannot bear fruit of itself, unless it abides in the vine, so neither can you, unless you abide in Me. I am the vine, you are the branches; he who abides in Me, and I in him, he bears much fruit; for apart from Me you can do nothing. If anyone does not abide in Me, he is thrown away as a branch, and dries up; and they gather them, and cast them into the fire, and they are burned. If you abide in Me, and My words abide in you, ask whatever you wish, and it shall be done for you.

John 15:4–7

3. Based on the above Scripture, what is required for us to bear fruit?

4. What type of fruit is Jesus talking about?

5. What does Jesus mean when He says if "My words abide in you"?

Just as the Father has loved Me, I have also loved you; abide in My love. If you keep My commandments, you will abide in My love; just as I have kept My Father's commandments, and abide in His love. *John 15:9–10*

6. Based on the above Scripture, what will ensure our abiding in Christ's love?

7. Read each Scripture below and note what it tells us about how to abide in Christ or the benefit of doing so.

The one who says he abides in Him ought himself to walk in the same manner as He walked.

1 John 2:6

The one who loves his brother abides in the light and there is no cause for stumbling in him.

1 John 2:10

And now, little children, abide in Him, so that when He appears, we may have confidence and not shrink away from Him in shame at His coming.

1 John 2:28

No one who abides in Him sins; no one who sins has seen Him or knows Him.

1 John 3:6

And the one who keeps His commandments abides in Him, and He in him. And we know by this that He abides in us, by the Spirit which He has given us.

1 John 3:24

No one has beheld God at any time; if we love one another, God abides in us, and His love is perfected in us. By this we know that we abide in Him and He in us, because He has given us of His Spirit.

1 John 4:12–13

Whoever confesses that Jesus is the Son of God, God abides in him, and he in God. And we have come to know and have believed the love which God has for us. God is love, and the one who abides in love abides in God, and God abides in him.

1 John 4:15–16

ABIDING WORKSHEET
FOR PERSONAL REFLECTION AND APPLICATION

Answer the questions below to assist in the development of the daily discipline of abiding.

QUESTIONS FOR YOUR CONSIDERATION	ANSWERS
HOW MUCH DAILY TIME SHOULD I SPEND IN PRAYER?	
HOW MUCH DAILY TIME SHOULD I SPEND IN BIBLE STUDY AND REFLECTION?	
WHAT TIME OR TIMES OF THE DAY WOULD WORK BEST FOR ME TO COMMUNE PRIVATELY WITH GOD?	
WILL DEVELOPING AND MAINTAINING THIS DISCIPLINE REQUIRE THAT I GIVE SOME THINGS UP? IF SO, WHAT?	
AM I WILLING TO MAKE THE TIME TO ABIDE IN CHRIST DAILY?	
IF SO, DESCRIBE THE DAILY DISCIPLINES I AM WILLING TO START TODAY.	

SCRIPTURES RELATED TO ABIDING

How Do We Abide in Christ?

He who eats My flesh and drinks My blood abides in Me, and I in him. *John 6:56*

Jesus therefore was saying to those Jews who had believed Him, "If you abide in My word, then you are truly disciples of Mine; and you shall know the truth, and the truth shall make you free." *John 8:31–32*

Abide in Me, and I in you. As the branch cannot bear fruit of itself, unless it abides in the vine, so neither can you, unless you abide in Me. I am the vine, you are the branches; he who abides in Me, and I in him, he bears much fruit; for apart from Me you can do nothing. If anyone does not abide in Me, he is thrown away as a branch, and dries up; and they gather them, and cast them into the fire, and they are burned. If you abide in Me, and My words abide in you, ask whatever you wish, and it shall be done for you. *John 15:4–7*

Just as the Father has loved Me, I have also loved you; abide in My love. If you keep My commandments, you will abide in My love; just as I have kept My Father's commandments, and abide in His love. *John 15:9–10*

The one who says he abides in Him ought himself to walk in the same manner as He walked. *1 John 2:6*

The one who loves his brother abides in the light and there is no cause for stumbling in him. *1 John 2:10*

I have written to you, fathers, because you know Him who has been from the beginning. I have written to you, young men, because you are strong, and the word of God abides in you, and you have overcome the evil one. *1 John 2:14*

And as for you, the anointing which you received from Him abides in you, and you have no need for any one to teach you; but as His anointing teaches you about all things, and is true and is not a lie, and just as it has taught you, you abide in Him. And now, little children, abide in Him, so that when He appears, we may have confidence and not shrink away from Him in shame at His coming. *1 John 2:27–28*

No one who abides in Him sins; no one who sins has seen Him or knows Him. *1 John 3:6*

And the one who keeps His commandments abides in Him, and He in him. And we know by this that He abides in us, by the Spirit which He has given us. *1 John 3:24*

No one has beheld God at any time; if we love one another, God abides in us, and His love is perfected in us. By this we know that we abide in Him and He in us, because He has given us of His Spirit. *1 John 4:12–13*

Whoever confesses that Jesus is the Son of God, God abides in him, and he in God. And we have come to know and have believed the love which God has for us. God is love, and the one who abides in love abides in God, and God abides in him. *1 John 4:15–16*

Scriptures Dealing with Prayer

But you, when you pray, go into your inner room, and when you have shut your door, pray to your Father who is in secret, and your Father who sees in secret will repay you. *Matt. 6:6*

Ask, and it shall be given to you; seek, and you shall find; knock, and it shall be opened to you. For every one who asks receives, and he who seeks finds, and to him who knocks it shall be opened. *Matt. 7:7–8*

And everything you ask in prayer, believing, you shall receive. *Matt. 21:22*

And He went a little beyond them, and fell on His face and prayed, saying, "My Father, if it is possible, let this cup pass from Me; yet not as I will, but as Thou wilt." *Matt. 26:39*

Therefore I say to you, all things for which you pray and ask, believe that you have received them, and they shall be granted you. And whenever you stand praying, forgive, if you have anything against anyone; so that your Father also who is in heaven may forgive you your transgressions. *Mark 11:24–25*

And whatever you ask in My name, that will I do, that the Father may be glorified in the Son. If you ask Me anything in My name, I will do it. *John 14:13–14*

You did not choose Me, but I chose you, and appointed you, that you should go and bear fruit, and that your fruit should remain, that whatever you ask of the Father in My name, He may give to you. *John 15:16*

And in that day you will ask Me no question. Truly, truly, I say to you, if you shall ask the Father for anything, He will give it to you in My name. Until now you have asked for nothing in My name; ask, and you will receive, that your joy may be made full. *John 16:23–24*

. . . always giving thanks for all things in the name of our Lord Jesus Christ to God, even the Father. *Eph. 5:20*

And whatever you do in word or deed, do all in the name of the Lord Jesus, giving thanks through Him to God the Father. *Col. 3:17*

Therefore, confess your sins to one another, and pray for one another, so that you may be healed. The effective prayer of a righteous man can accomplish much. Elijah was a man with a nature like ours, and he prayed earnestly that it might not rain; and it did not rain on the earth for three years and six months. And he prayed again, and the sky poured rain, and the earth produced its fruit. *James 5:16–18*

Scriptures Related to Meditation

Let my meditation be pleasing to Him; As for me, I shall be glad in the Lord. *Ps. 104:34*

Thy word I have treasured in my heart, That I may not sin against Thee. *Ps. 119:11*

I will meditate on Thy precepts, And regard Thy ways. I shall delight in Thy statutes; I shall not forget Thy word. *Ps. 119:15–16*

God's Word as a Resource for Knowing God's Will

Therefore every one who hears these words of Mine, and acts upon them, may be compared to a wise man, who built his house upon the rock. And the rain descended, and the floods came, and the winds blew, and burst against that house; and yet it did not fall, for it had been founded upon the rock. *Matt. 7:24–25*

But He answered and said to them, "My mother and My brothers are these who hear the word of God and do it."   *Luke 8:21*

But He said, "On the contrary, blessed are those who hear the word of God, and observe it."   *Luke 11:28*

And you do not have His word abiding in you, for you do not believe Him whom He sent.   *John 5:38*

Jesus therefore was saying to those Jews who had believed Him, "If you abide in My word, then you are truly disciples of Mine."   *John 8:31*

If you abide in Me, and My words abide in you, ask whatever you wish, and it shall be done for you.   *John 15:4–7*

So faith comes from hearing, and hearing by the word of Christ.   *Rom. 10:17*

And take the helmet of salvation, and the sword of the Spirit, which is the word of God.   *Eph. 6:17*

Let the word of Christ richly dwell within you, with all wisdom teaching and admonishing one another with psalms and hymns and spiritual songs, singing with thankfulness in your hearts to God.   *Col. 3:16*

For the word of God is living and active and sharper than any two-edged sword, and piercing as far as the division of soul and spirit, of both joints and marrow, and able to judge the thoughts and intentions of the heart.   *Heb. 4:12*

For you have been born again not of seed which is perishable but imperishable, that is, through the living and abiding word of God.   *1 Pet. 1:23*

And He is clothed with a robe dipped in blood; and His name is called The Word of God.   *Rev. 19:13*

Seeking God's Will

But seek first His kingdom and His righteousness; and all these things shall be added to you.   *Matt. 6:33*

Ask, and it shall be given to you; seek, and you shall find; knock, and it shall be opened to you.   *Matt. 7:7*

CHAPTER FOURTEEN

WITNESSING: AFFECTING OTHERS FOR CHRIST

CHRISTIAN PRINCIPLE: WITNESS	AA'S STEP TWELVE	CHRISTIAN ADAPTATION
You are the light of the world. A city set on a hill cannot be hidden. Nor do men light a lamp, and put it under the peck-measure, but on the lampstand; and it gives light to all who are in the house. Let your light shine before men in such a way that they may see your good works, and glorify your Father who is in heaven. *Matt. 5:14–16*	Having had a spiritual awakening as the result of these steps, we tried to carry this message to alcoholics, and to practice these principles in all our affairs.	Having been changed by Christ, we now make ourselves available to be used by Him in the lives of others.

Pictures from my youth reveal a lifelong struggle—overeating. Since I was a young child I have constantly struggled to lose weight. Years ago I read a diet book that I found extremely helpful. I followed its advice and surprisingly lost the weight I desired.

I would proclaim the diet's effectiveness whenever possible. My purpose was simple—I wanted others to experience the benefits that I had.

Similarly, the benefits of our relationship with Christ are to be shared with others. While Jesus walked the earth, He proclaimed Himself: "the light of the world."[1] He was God's representa- tive, providing all interested parties the opportunity to see God's character, to understand the difference between light and darkness and to follow Him. He boldly proclaimed His purpose and provided all those who heard Him the opportunity to bask in His light.

His actions supported His words. He expressed His love to all types of people—even people who didn't love Him. He called sinners to repentance, He sought and saved the lost, He comforted the brokenhearted, and He invited the rich and the poor alike to Himself.

Jesus' ministry continues today through us. He now proclaims that "we" are the "light of the

---

1. John 9:5

world"[2] and as Christ's servants, we are called to represent Him in a desperate world filled with desperate people. We are His ambassadors entrusted with an incredible responsibility to share His love with others. Our effort to affect others for Christ is called witnessing.

Witnessing is sharing God's love with others. Each day we reflect His love in a hurting world. Daily we consider whom should we pray for, whom we can help, how we can minister to others the love Christ has ministered to us. As we extend His love to others, we project His light into a dark world—we become His witnesses.

Christians who have surrendered themselves to Christ have both a gift and a responsibility.

Our gift is a relationship with God. Through Christ's death we have been forgiven, restored, and reconciled to God. Sin's separating power has been marvelously replaced with God's mercy. We have been empowered to repent of destructive behaviors and enabled to become like Jesus. We now have hope for the future, a sense of purpose for our lives, and a peace "which surpasses all comprehension."[3] All this God has graciously given to us.

Our responsibility is to share this incredible gift with others, to proclaim that Christ is available to them, forgiveness is within reach, and God can do for them what He has done for us. Freely we have received and freely we should give.[4]

We witness Christ's love for others in two intimately connected ways—by what we say and do. Integrity between our words and deeds is indis-pensable to credible witnessing. In fact, our actions often speak louder then our words, particularly if they contradict our proclaimed faith.

A slimmer body had to support my claims about the diet I referred to at the start of the chapter. Had I said, "This is a great diet. It really works," yet gained weight, my claims would have been questionable. If I publicly had eaten foods the diet prohibited, my claim would also have been ignored. Practicing what I preached was essential to the credibility of my claims. Similarly, our Christian witness must be supported by a lifestyle consistent with our message that includes what the Bible calls good works.

Jesus' ministry was practical. He didn't just talk about God's love, He modeled it. He healed the sick, comforted the afflicted, fed the hungry, and loved and accepted society's rejected. He ministered to children as well as adults, to men as well as women, to the rich as well as the poor. He was never aloof or unconcerned but was constantly seeking opportunities to affect others for God's sake.

As followers of Christ, should we do anything less? If His Spirit directs us, will He not lead us in a similar way? If God has transformed our greed into generosity, He will invariably ask us to contribute to needy people and worthy causes. If He has put mercy in our heart, we will naturally seek out hurting people to comfort. Just as He ministered to those in need, He will direct us to do the same.

Ministering to others has a dual purpose. Jesus tells us that when we minister to people in

---

2. Matt. 5:14
3. Phil. 4:7
4. Matt. 10:8

need, we are ministering to Christ Himself. This is an odd but important truth. Consider these words of His.

> "For I was hungry, and you gave Me something to eat; I was thirsty, and you gave Me drink; I was a stranger, and you invited Me in; naked, and you clothed Me; I was sick, and you visited Me; I was in prison, and you came to Me." Then the righteous will answer Him, saying, "Lord, when did we see You hungry, and feed You, or thirsty, and give You drink? And when did we see You a stranger, and invite You in, or naked, and clothe You? And when did we see You sick, or in prison, and come to You?" And the King will answer and say to them, "Truly I say to you, to the extent that you did it to one of these brothers of Mine, even the least of them, you did it to Me."[5]

When we feed the hungry, clothe the naked, or visit the sick, we are ministering not just to hurting individuals, but also to Jesus. As Christ's people we must actively seek opportunities to minister to Him by ministering to people in need.

Recognizing our need to be of service, we patiently await His directives to affect the lives of others. The specific nature of our good works will vary from individual to individual based on our gifts, abilities, circumstances, and Christ's purpose for our lives. He will undoubtedly show us whom to minister to and in what fashion as we prayerfully seek His will.

Our witness will invariably include telling others how Jesus has affected our lives. Our changed character and good works will certainly provide such opportunities. As God's ambassadors, we express to others the incredible value of our relationship with Him. As Peter says, we should always be ready to make a defense to everyone who asks us to give an account for the hope Christ has given us.[6]

How we share our faith is important. Never share your faith in an arrogant, self-righteous, or condemning manner. This will almost always have the opposite effect of what God intends. Arguments are rarely helpful and should be avoided. Always share your faith with the same love and grace that God has provided you through Christ. Our goal is not to judge or condemn others but out of a loving interest for their well-being we thoughtfully, gently, and reverently let others know about Christ's love for them.

Different people will respond differently. Some will be offended, some will be uninterested, but others will be attracted to genuine Christianity because countless people are hurting and looking for answers to life. They are searching for hope, serenity, peace, joy, and a sense of purpose. If Christ's love dwells within us, it will certainly make an impression on a number of people God puts in our lives.

Perhaps the most effective way we proclaim Christ is by describing to others what God has done in our lives. How He met us and changed us and is with us. Not everyone values the sayings of Christ. Many people have contempt for organized religion. But few can take issue with

---

5. Matt. 25:35–40
6. 1 Pet. 3:15

changed lives. Describing how Christ has changed you will often have a great impact.

Witnessing also brings us closer to Christ. When we are ministering to others, we sense His presence in a unique and powerful way. Jesus proclaims that where He is, His servants will also be.[7] Because Jesus is in the love business, the ministry business, the forgiveness business, so, too, will His servants. If we follow Him in serving the practical and spiritual needs of others, we experience His intimate presence in a way that's difficult to describe.

This has been my experience. I have never experienced Christ's presence more powerfully and personally then when I minister to the spiritual needs of hurting inmates in jails. Why? Because nothing has changed! Just as Jesus was present two thousand years ago, inviting the weak and brokenhearted to Him, He still is today. As we affect the lives of others for His sake, we sense His presence in a way that's indescribable.

Finally, witnessing provides us with an exciting sense of purpose. Nothing is more satisfying than the realization that we are in partnership with God in the lives of others. As God uses us to help others, we know why we are here. Not simply to survive, or satisfy us, but to be God's agents to accomplish His will in the lives of others. As you determine to follow Christ in all areas of your life, may He strengthen you to be used mightily in the lives of others.

---

7. John 12:26

WITNESSING WORKSHEET
FOR GROUP DISCUSSION AND PERSONAL REFLECTION

1. Who in your life has influenced your faith?

2. What was it about this person that influenced you: what they said, what they did, or both? (Describe what was said or done.)

3. Based on the following Scripture, what influence will good works often have on others?

Let your light shine before men in such a way that they may see your good works, and glorify your Father who is in heaven.   *Matt. 5:16*

4. How has your faith influenced your relationships with others?

5. What are the implications of the following verse?

Every one therefore who shall confess Me before men, I will also confess him before My Father who is in heaven. But whoever shall deny Me before men, I will also deny him before My Father who is in heaven.

Matt. 10:32–33

6. Read Acts 22 and answer the following questions.

What elements of his testimony did Paul choose to share?

What was the outcome of his sharing?

Do you think the mob's angry response was a surprise to Paul? Explain.

In light of the potential danger, why did Paul share his testimony?

WITNESSING WORKSHEET
FOR PERSONAL REFLECTION ONLY

1. Jesus' ministry was characterized by helping people who were weak and rejected. Matthew 25 suggests that His people will continue in this manner. Do you feel that Jesus might be leading you to minister to any particular group of people; for example, youth, infants, poor, incarcerated, depressed, addicted. If yes, what makes you think so?

2. Fear often inhibits our willingness to confess our faith to others. Do you have any fears about professing your faith? If so, what are they?

3. The Apostles in Acts 4 prayed for power to confess their faith in Christ despite cruel opposition. Would a similar prayer be helpful to you?

SCRIPTURES RELATED TO WITNESSING

We, Through Christ, Are the Light of the World

Nor do men light a lamp, and put it under the peck-measure, but on the lampstand; and it gives light to all who are in the house. Let your light shine before men in such a way that they may see your good works, and glorify your Father who is in heaven. *Matt. 5:15–16*

The night is almost gone, and the day is at hand. Let us therefore lay aside the deeds of darkness and put on the armor of light. Let us behave properly as in the day, not in carousing and drunkenness, not in sexual promiscuity and sensuality, not in strife and jealousy. But put on the Lord Jesus Christ, and make no provision for the flesh in regard to its lusts. *Rom. 13:12–14*

For you were formerly darkness, but now you are light in the Lord; walk as children of light. *Eph. 5:8*

Prove yourselves to be blameless and innocent, children of God above reproach in the midst of a crooked and perverse generation, among whom you appear as lights in the world, holding fast the word of life, so that in the day of Christ I may have cause to glory because I did not run in vain nor toil in vain. *Phil. 2:15–16*

And this is the message we have heard from Him and announce to you, that God is light, and in Him there is no darkness at all. If we say that we have fellowship with Him and yet walk in the darkness, we lie and do not practice the truth; but if we walk in the light as He Himself is in the light, we have fellowship with one another, and the blood of Jesus His Son cleanses us from all sin. *1 John 1:5–7*

Good Works as a Vital Element of Genuine Christianity

Let your light shine before men in such a way that they may see your good works, and glorify your Father who is in heaven. *Matt. 5:16*

For we are His workmanship, created in Christ Jesus for good works, which God prepared beforehand, that we should walk in them. *Eph. 2:10*

. . . but rather by means of good works, as befits women making a claim to godliness. *1 Tim. 2:10*

Likewise also, deeds that are good are quite evident, and those which are otherwise cannot be concealed. *1 Tim. 5:25*

Instruct them to do good, to be rich in good works, to be generous and ready to share. *1 Tim. 6:18*

. . . that the man of God may be adequate, equipped for every good work. *2 Tim. 3:17*

In all things show yourself to be an example of good deeds, with purity in doctrine, dignified . . . *Titus 2:7*

. . . who gave Himself for us, that He might redeem us from every lawless deed and purify for Himself a people for His own possession, zealous for good deeds. *Titus 2:14*

This is a trustworthy statement; and concerning these things I want you to speak confidently, so that those who have believed God may be careful to engage in good deeds. These things are good and profitable for men. *Titus 3:8*

And let our people also learn to engage in good deeds to meet pressing needs, that they may not be unfruitful. *Titus 3:14*

Let us consider how to stimulate one another to love and good deeds. *Heb. 10:24*

Keep your behavior excellent among the Gentiles, so that in the thing in which they slander you as evildoers, they may on account of your good deeds, as they observe them, glorify God in the day of visitation. *1 Pet. 2:12*

We Must Tell Others about Christ

And He said to them, "Go into all the world and preach the gospel to all creation." *Mark 16:15*

Therefore if any man is in Christ, he is a new creature; the old things passed away; behold, new things have come. Now all these things are from God, who reconciled us to Himself through Christ, and gave us the ministry of reconciliation, namely, that God was in Christ reconciling the world to Himself, not counting their trespasses against them, and He has committed to us the word of reconciliation.

Therefore, we are ambassadors for Christ, as though God were entreating through us; we beg you on behalf of Christ, be reconciled to God. *2 Cor. 5:17–20*

But you are a chosen race, a royal priesthood, a holy nation, a people for God's own possession, that you may proclaim the excellencies of Him who has called you out of darkness into His marvelous light. *1 Pet. 2:9*

ABOUT THE AUTHOR

Saul Selby is an ordained minister and a licensed drug and alcohol counselor. Since 1983 Selby has concurrently worked professionally with addicts and ministered to inmates. He is employed as both the director of clinical operations at Hazelden in Center City, and the executive director of missionary evangelism to corrections. Originally from New York City, Selby currently resides in Minnesota with his wife, Karen, and two children. His life was radically changed in 1980 when he made a commitment to Christ while in treatment for alcohol and drug addiction. He has written a number of pamphlets including *A Look at Cross-Addiction* and *The Voice of Addiction*. He regularly makes presentations on topics related to Christian living and recovery.